Praise for *Happy Meat, Humane A...*

"Society is gradually coming to terms with the harsh realities of animal agriculture, as long-hidden truths about the industry's practices and the dark places where animals have been hidden for decades are being exposed. In response to mounting scrutiny, the industry claims that it can improve its operations and produce 'happy' meat and 'humane' animal products with adjustments to its production practices. However, as Peter Marsh's book, *Happy Meat, Humane Animal Research, and Other Myths* reveals, there is a fundamental ethical dilemma to confining and killing animals for human consumption that cannot be solved with minor changes to an inherently cruel system. Regardless of the labels on the packaging or rationalizations on the product websites, the truth remains: there is no humane way to justify the exploitation of animals for food."—**Hope Bohanec**, author of *The Ultimate Betrayal: Is There Happy Meat?* and editor of *The Humane Hoax: Essays Exposing the Myth of Happy Meat, Humane Dairy and Ethical Eggs*

"In *Happy Meat, Humane Animal Research, and Other Myths*, Marsh challenges us to confront the cognitive dissonance at the core of our treatment of animals. Essential reading for anyone who has ever wondered why kind people participate in cruel practices."—**Jess Bugg**, author, *You Had to Be There: Thoughts of Ecological Grief in the Anthropocene*

"What does it mean to be humane? We accept the definition as being characterized by kindness, mercy, or compassion as well as pertaining to a human. People might have intentions of being humane, but the reality is many humans commit great atrocities against each other and to animals and nature. Whether it's in research or raising animals for food, when there's suffering involved, can the activity truly be called humane? In *Happy Meat, Humane Animal Research, and Other Myths*, Peter Marsh gives us the proof that what we often call humane is not what we have defined it to mean. It's a paradox. Marsh connects the dots between the cruel way people treat other people and how animals are made to experience pain and suffering at our human hands. Marsh offers hope with suggestions on how we can overcome our prejudices and become kind, compassionate, humane human beings."—**Caryn Hartglass**, Co-Founder and President, Responsible Eating And Living

"You will love to read Peter Marsh's *Happy Meat, Humane Animal Research, and Other Myths*. The book will supply you with state-of-the-art facts, figures, and arguments that will empower you to defeat the nonsense thrown at you by animal exploiters and their apologists. So read it and be prepared, for every one of us is an advocate for our animal cousins. Every one of us needs to be armed and equipped to knock down the exploiters and stand over them for our animal cousins.

Marsh's book has an unintended benefit: It shows the lengths to which exploiters must go to lie and deny about their work. For me, this is a good thing, because it shows that there is a universal human affinity for our animal cousins. We have good instincts, but our dominant human supremacist worldview beats them down with lies, denials, and all sorts of desensitization so that people can 'enjoy' the benefits of animal slavery without having to have unpleasant thoughts and feelings."—**Jim Mason**, author, *An Unnatural Order: The Roots of our Destruction of Nature*

HAPPY MEAT, HUMANE ANIMAL RESEARCH, AND OTHER MYTHS

How People Harm Animals and Still Live with Themselves

Peter Marsh

Lantern Publishing & Media ● Woodstock & Brooklyn, NY

2025
Lantern Publishing & Media
PO Box 1350
Woodstock, NY 12498
www.lanternpm.org

Copyright © 2025 Peter Marsh

All rights reserved. No part of this book may be reproduced, stored in a retrieval system, or transmitted in any form or by any means, electronic, mechanical, photocopying, recording, or otherwise, without the written permission of Lantern Publishing & Media.

Printed in the United States of America

Library of Congress Cataloging-in-Publication Data

Names: Marsh, Peter, author.
Title: Happy meat, humane animal research and other myths : how people harm
    animals and still live with themselves / Peter Marsh.
Description: Woodstock, NY : Lantern Publishing & Media, [2025] | Includes
    bibliographical references.
Identifiers: LCCN 2024022880 | ISBN 9781590567418 (paperback) | ISBN
    9781590567425 (epub)
Subjects: LCSH: Animal welfare. | Food animals—Moral and ethical aspects. |
    Violence—Moral and ethical aspects.
Classification: LCC HV4708 .M364 2025 | DDC 179/.3—dc23/eng/20250118
LC record available at https://lccn.loc.gov/2024022880

Contents

Acknowledgments vii
Introduction ix

1. The Exonerative Use of Language:
   Nazis Called the Group That Murdered
   Institutionalized People the Charitable
   Foundation for Institutional Care 1

2. Negate the Harm: Auschwitz:
   The Hidden Death Camp 7

3. Denigrate the Victims:
   "They're *Untermenschen* (subhuman)" 15

4. Disparage the Critics:
   "The Abolitionists Are Hypocrites" 21

5. Displace Responsibility:
   Adolph Eichmann: "Like Pontius Pilate,
   I felt free of guilt" 25

6. Diffuse Responsibility:
   Nazi Doctor at Auschwitz: "I am a victim of
   the environment, no less than the inmates" 29

7. The Exonerative Use of Comparisons:
   "At least we didn't kill any children" 33

8. Moral Justification:
   "Shooting the children soothed my conscience" 35

9. The Interconnection of Prejudices
   Against People and Animals 47

10. Overcoming Interconnected Prejudices 61

Appendix: The Omnivore's Moral Dilemmas 71

Bibliography 81
Notes 105

About the Author
About the Publisher

Acknowledgments

Many thanks to Jim Mason, Peter Singer, Troon Harrison, and João Graca for their generosity in reviewing all or parts of the manuscript and offering suggestions about how to improve it. Thanks, also, to Albert Bandura for his many insights about how people use methods of moral disengagement to feel better about harming others and to Kristof Dhont, Gordon Hodson, João Graca and their colleagues for research about the interconnection of different forms of prejudice, including prejudice against animals. And, most of all, to Roxanne for sharing this project with me.

Introduction

"We kill animals for food; we use them as experimental subjects in laboratories; we exploit them as sources of raw materials such as leather and wool; we keep them as work animals—the list goes on and on. These practices are to our advantage, and we intend to continue them. Thus, when we think about what the animals are like, we are motivated to conceive of them in ways that are compatible with treating them in these ways. If animals are conceived as intelligent, sensitive beings, these ways of treating them might seem monstrous. So humans have reason to resist thinking of them as intelligent or sensitive."

—**James Rachels**, *Created from Animals: The Moral Implications of Darwinism* (Oxford: Oxford University Press, 1990), 129.

In his 2006 bestseller, *The Omnivore's Dilemma*, Michael Pollan shared how he became a vegetarian, if only briefly. It all began when he read part of Peter Singer's *Animal Liberation* while enjoying a medium-rare steak at a steakhouse. He finished eating the steak, but Singer's ideas about the ethics of eating animals continued to trouble him.[1] He read the work of others who criticized eating meat, found their arguments convincing, and decided to try being a vegetarian.

From the outset, though, he loved eating meat so much that he was a "reluctant" vegetarian.[2] After a short time, he convinced himself that although it was unethical to eat animals raised under the nightmarish conditions on factory farms, eating "happy meat" from other farms was different. Two ideas soothed his conscience: that predation was "deeply woven into the fabric of nature" and that animals raised for food have entered into a symbiotic bargain in which people provide them with protection and food and they provide people with their flesh.[3] As will be discussed in this book, defenders of slavery and male supremacy both made similar claims. They said that slavery and the subordination of women were natural.[4] They also claimed that slavery and men's domination of women were mutually beneficial bargains in which slaves and women enjoyed great benefits.[5] These justifications, of course, were wrong.

Pollan's are, too. When he discussed whether it's alright for us to be carnivores, because some other animals are, he asked readers, "Do you really want to base your moral code on the natural order? Murder and rape are natural, too."[6,7] Predation is also a big part of nature. And farmed animals haven't agreed to any "bargain with humanity."[8,9] If they had, farmers wouldn't need to confine them so carefully to prevent them from escaping.

As he wrestled with the moral questions raised by eating meat, Pollan commented that he pitied vegetarians as naïve dreamers ignorant about the workings of the natural world.[10] He also mentioned that while he was helping slaughter some chickens on a farm he visited, the chickens appeared to be completely unaware that they were about to be killed, and he "took solace in their seeming obliviousness."[11]

All of this would probably seem familiar to Albert Bandura, a psychologist who devoted his career to understanding the many ways people can disengage their moral values and avoid feeling guilty about doing something wrong. He explained how, among other methods of moral disengagement, we can justify what we've done by saying—as Pollan did—that it wasn't wrong in the first place or at least wasn't as bad as some other things people do or that no one was really hurt by it or those who were hurt aren't worth our concern.[12]

Bandura's ideas about moral disengagement have led to valuable insights about many forms of mass violence, from wartime atrocities and terrorism to genocide.[13] This book applies them to another form of widespread violence—violence against animals. At an early age, we learn that it's wrong to harm animals, and most people are upset if they see an animal suffering or being mistreated. We want to treat animals humanely, yet most of us harm them directly or indirectly every day.[14]

This book is about how people harm animals and use methods of disengagement to avoid feeling guilty about it. Attempting to set themselves apart from the appalling conditions in which animals are raised on factory farms, Michael Pollan and many other people believe it isn't morally troublesome to eat meat from "happy" farms where the owners say chickens take dust baths in tree-lined meadows, pigs root around with other pigs whose company they enjoy, and calves graze contentedly with their mothers in lush pastures. Along the same lines, the Happy Egg Company says the eggs it sells come from happy hens free to roam year-round through gently wooded hillsides. And the California dairy industry promoted an iconic series of ads telling how great cheese comes from happy California cows.

Other farmers use more subtle forms of "humane washing," saying that the animals on their farms are *cage-free* or *free-range* or *pasture-raised* or *Certified Humane*. This book discusses why the animals on these farms may be less miserable than those on factory farms but still aren't happy.[15] It also explains why Certified Humane farms should instead be called Certified Less Inhumane.

Scientists who use animals in their research employ their own form of humane washing. Although they describe their research as humane, this book discusses why their experiments aren't *humane* under any reasonable definition of the word and can often be more accurately described as *cruel*.

Some researchers claim that their research is justified because the animals they experiment upon have no sense of morality.[16] In this book, you'll learn about studies that found that rats and mice—the animals used most often in experiments—behave empathically and altruistically toward each other.

* * *

We need to understand how methods of moral disengagement work. They allow us to disregard our own values, leaving us morally adrift. Understanding how they do that will make it easier to dismantle them.

It may help to consider an example. During World War II, some German police officers who killed infants and small children during massacres of Polish Jews said that killing the children was humane because it prevented them from suffering a slow death after other officers had killed their mothers (a form of moral disengagement Bandura called *moral justification*).[17] Those who killed the mothers told themselves that at least they hadn't killed any children (a method of disengagement he called *advantageous comparison*).[18] Other officers killed both children and their mothers and felt they were free of blame because they were just following orders (*displacement of responsibility*).[19] All of these men had one thing in common: They used moral disengagement to feel better about behaving in reprehensible ways.

Each of the first eight chapters in this book will tell how people harm animals in the ways James Rachels mentioned in the quotation that opened this chapter and use one particular method of disengagement to absolve themselves from that harm. Along the way, readers will find out the following:

- Why it's wrong to take the lives of animals living on "happy farms," especially if their lives are filled with happiness.
- Why researchers identify the animals they use in their experiments with numbers instead of names.
- How some research scientists hide the suffering they inflict on the animals they use while others are less covert, openly modifying animals to suffer throughout their lives from illness or disease.

The final two chapters will discuss why many of the myths people have recently created to justify the way we treat animals—including the Myth of Happy Meat and the Myth of Humane Animal Research—are like the more benevolent myths that modern sexists and racists use to legitimize the ways they treat their victims. These chapters also discuss how different forms of prejudice are interconnected and why we won't be able to eradicate other forms of prejudice without eradicating prejudice against animals, too.

It turns out that our exceptional mental abilities are both a blessing and a curse. They give with one hand and can take away with the other. They make it possible for us to have profound moral insights but then to disregard them when that serves our purpose. Fortunately, they also allow us to see through these "sleights of mind." This book will tell how we can do that and dispel the prejudices that have caused so much harm to us, the planet we live on, and the animals with whom we share it.

≈ 1 ≈

The Exonerative Use of Language

Nazis Called the Group That Murdered Institutionalized People the Charitable Foundation for Institutional Care

> "By camouflaging pernicious activities in innocent or sanitizing parlance, the activities lose much of their repugnancy."
>
> —**Albert Bandura**, "Moral Disengagement in the Perpetration of Inhumanities," *Personality and Social Psychology Review* 3(3)(1999), 195.

In the early days of World War II, the Nazis systematically killed more than 70,000 handicapped people who lived in state hospitals, nursing homes, and asylums, people they considered "unworthy of life."[1] They called the group that organized and carried out these murders the Charitable Foundation for Institutional Care, although it provided no care to anyone, whether in an institution or anywhere else.[2] When they used euphemisms to hide their brutality, the Nazis were employing one of the most versatile methods of moral disengagement—the exonerative use of language. Those who harm others commonly use euphemisms and other language to hide, misrepresent, or even justify the harm they inflict. Following are some examples.

Meat producers often disguise their violence with comforting language. When they cut off part of a chicken's beak, they refer to it as *beak trimming* or *beak conditioning,* making it seem like a spa treatment; and when they amputate part of a turkey or a chicken's toes, they call it *toe clipping* or *toenail clipping* as if it were part of a pedicure.[3] They often use linguistic camouflage when they kill the animals, too. They say the animals are *processed,* not *slaughtered,* and the place where they're killed isn't a *slaughterhouse*, it's a *processing plant.*[4]

To make some of their products seem more appetizing, meat producers call them *pork, beef,* or *mutton,* not the flesh of pigs, cattle, or sheep. As one woman explained when she received back packages marked GOAT MEAT after having brought a goat to slaughter, "This has a sort of 'turn off' ring to it. It angered me a little too because goat meat is a perfectly respectable meat. It is called chevon, like PIG MEAT is called pork—like COW MEAT is called beef. A simple request next time brought back beautifully stamped packages of CHEVON CHOPS, CHEVON STEAKS, GROUND CHEVON, etc."[5]

Scientists who conduct experiments on animals also use innocent-sounding language to camouflage what they do.[6] When researchers deprive animals of nutrition in an experiment, they often refer to them as *fasting*, implying that the animals decided to forego food. One group of researchers referred to the metal chairs in which they shackled baboons—sometimes for weeks on end—as *housing.*[7] Another group of researchers prevented rats from sleeping by suspending them over water on a disc that began to rotate in one direction and, if they fell asleep, sent them into the water unless they woke up and moved in the opposite direction. Authors of the study said the animals *resided* on the plastic disc, suggesting they had made it their home.[8]

Sometimes scientists who used a disc-over-water apparatus didn't wait until the animals died from sleep deprivation to finish their experiment. Instead, they said they *sacrificed* the animals when their death appeared imminent.[9] It shouldn't be surprising that scientists who kill the animals they've used in experiments often come up with words like *sacrifice* to describe what they've done. People who take a life are understandably reluctant to describe it as *killing*. The Nazis referred to the murders they were committing as *Sonderbehandlung* (special treatment) or one of many other innocuous-sounding terms to avoid using the German word for *kill*.[10] *Sacrifice* isn't the only euphemism researchers use to avoid saying they've killed the animals they used. They say they've *dispatched, terminated, exsanguinated,* or *put down* individual animals and *depopulated* groups of animals, a process they sometimes refer to as *housecleaning*.[11, 12]

Hunters, fishermen, and meat producers employ a different strategy to disguise killing; they borrow a term from plant-based agriculture and refer to taking an animal's life as *harvesting* the animal, suggesting that disemboweling and dismembering an animal is like cutting wheat or picking fruit from a tree.[13] As one anthrozoologist put it:

> [v]erbal concealment crops up in most areas of animal exploitation. We speak of the "harvest of the seas" as if fish and shellfish were analogous to wheat and barley, and in the fur trade "pelts" are "harvested" rather than animals flayed. It is even tempting to suggest that much of the technical jargon employed by scientists who experiment on animals is simply an elaborate euphemism, a method of disguising the animal's affinity with humans, and so promote detachment.[14]

* * *

In some cases, perpetrators even use exonerative language to justify the harm they inflict. People who take an animal's life sometimes say they've euthanized the animal. *Euthanasia* is derived from Greek words meaning "good death." It's supposed to mean ending an animal's life when that's in the animal's best interests and using humane techniques to bring about a rapid loss of consciousness with minimal pain and distress.[15]

In 2020, an American meat producer used the term to justify roasting more than 200,000 healthy pigs and piglets to death by sealing barns where they were kept, turning up the heat, shutting off the ventilation, and increasing the humidity in the barns with steam generators. They found that most of the pigs stopped squealing about fifty-five minutes after the temperature in the barn reached 130° F. In many cases, though, the *time to silent,* as the experts called it, was well over an hour.[16] The producer claimed it had acted ethically and provided the pigs with a good death. As a spokesperson explained, "Being forced to euthanize pigs is a devastating last resort. If our pigs can't go to market, barns become overcrowded and to us it is unethical to let an animal suffer."[17, 18]

As George Orwell noted, sometimes people use jargon when they need to name something but don't want to call up a mental picture of it.[19] Researchers commonly use technical language to do that. When they blind an animal by surgically removing his or her eyes, researchers sometimes refer to the animal as *visually deprived*; when they intentionally scald an animal, they say the animal suffered a *thermal injury*; and when they starve an animal to death, they say the animal died of *nutritional insufficiency*. Often, the use of this jargon is intentional. Editors at the *Journal of Experimental Medicine* advised researchers to sanitize their reports by substituting *fasting* for *starving,* *hemorrhaging* for *bleeding,* and *intoxicant* for *poison.*[20]

Researchers have also developed innocent-sounding jargon to camouflage the injuries they inflict. They refer to burns or electric shocks as *aversive stimuli*. When they cut a dog's vocal cords, they call it *debarking*. When they sew an animal's eyelids shut after surgically removing his or her eyes, they say the animal has undergone a *bilateral lid suture*, suggesting that it's a form of medical treatment.

Meat producers also use jargon to hide the injuries they cause. When they say they've killed a chicken by *cervical dislocation*, it means they've snapped his or her neck. When they grab piglets by the hind legs and kill them by bashing their heads against a hard surface, they call the technique *manually applied blunt force trauma*.

As Orwell also noted, the misuse of language can corrupt thought.[21] It can do more than that. When we use it to hide, minimize, or excuse our wrongdoing, we corrupt ourselves, too.

⁓ 2 ⁓

Negate the Harm

Auschwitz: The Hidden Death Camp

"As long as harmful effects are out of sight and out of mind there is no moral issue to contend with because no perceived harm has been done."

—**Albert Bandura**, *Moral Disengagement: How People Do Harm and Live with Themselves* (New York: Worth Publishers, 2016), 3.

The Nazis were content to conceal their routine violence with euphemisms and code words. They realized, though, that linguistic camouflage wouldn't be sufficient to hide the mass murders they planned to commit at extermination centers, so they actually hid death camps. They located one near a remote town in southern Poland so it could be hidden among several slave labor camps in the area.[1] The disguise worked. They murdered hundreds of thousands of people at Auschwitz-Birkenau before the Allies realized it was a death camp.[2]

Most intensive meat producers also place their production facilities in remote areas.[3] They keep pigs and poultry in windowless buildings that look more like warehouses than barns. Slaughterhouses, too, are usually hidden from public view on the outskirts of towns, and the animals' trip there tends to be made surreptitiously.[4] This is fine with most people; they don't like to be reminded that the chicken or leg of lamb they had for a Sunday meal was once a warm-blooded, sentient life form like themselves.[5] They prefer remaining "willfully blind"[6] to what goes on in modern meat production operations and accept producers' representations that their operations are like Old MacDonald's farm despite clear evidence to the contrary.[7, 8]

Meat producers hide the harm they inflict in other ways, too. As mentioned in the previous chapter, they call their products *pork*, *bacon*, *veal*, or *beef*, and they sell them in neat, bloodless packages because people are less inclined to buy products that remind them that meat comes from killing animals.[9]

Scientists who use animals in their experiments hide the harm they inflict in similar ways. They usually don't identify where their laboratories are located and tightly restrict access to them. Security was so tight at one facility that someone who worked there said, "To get into the animal room is like getting into Fort Knox."[10, 11] Researchers also limit access to information about their experiments because they're afraid members of the public wouldn't understand why they're being performed or activists would misrepresent what they involve.[12] In one laboratory where tubing carried blood between one dog and the severed head of another, experimenters closed the blinds on the windows, concerned that a critic might take photographs of the experiment with a long-distance lens and use the photos to discredit the lab.[13] Many people aren't familiar with the experiments and want it to stay that way, worried they'll be disturbed by details about the animals' suffering.[14] When researchers hide the harm they inflict and members of the public hide *from* the harm, it creates a "don't ask, don't tell" conspiracy of silence like that between meat producers and consumers.[15, 16]

Avoiding Information About Animal Suffering

Thinking about others' suffering, whether the others are human or animal, is difficult. One coping mechanism with which most readers are probably familiar in the human context is avoidance. . . . According to Shaw et al. (citation omitted), feeling empathy for another person motivates us to help, and yet sometimes helping can be quite costly in terms of, for example, energy, time, or resources that we may be unprepared to give. Also, the feeling of empathy itself can be taxing, and so people may want to avoid feeling it (citation omitted). A similar dynamic likely occurs when people focus on animal suffering; people feel empathy or distress, and yet because responding effectively seems to require changes that people may be unable or unprepared to give (e.g., diet change) many cope by avoiding the challenging information. This avoidance is easy, given that animal processing typically occurs well away from public places and accurate complete information about it is not typically widely disseminated (citation omitted).

Lynne M. Jackson, *The Psychology of Prejudice: From Attitudes to Social Action*, second edition (Washington, D.C.: American Psychological Association, 2020), 198.

Besides hiding it, animal researchers often discount the harm that animals suffer when used in their experiments. They say that even though animals can experience pain, they don't suffer from it nearly as much as we do. They believe that our ability to imagine the future makes our suffering much more intense than anything other animals can experience.[17] Such claims bring to mind the defenders of slavery, who said that Black people experience pain far less intensely than whites. For instance, in 1799 an American physician reported that "they are void of sensibility to a surprising degree.... They bear surgical operations much better than white people; and what would be a cause of unsupportable pain to a white man, a negro would almost disregard."[18]

The capacities said to make human suffering worse—our memory and sense of time—may actually make it less intense. When we have a headache, for example, we may be able to cope with it by anticipating when the pain will end based on previous experiences with headaches or analgesic medication.[19] And a person undergoing brain surgery may look forward to their ultimate recovery, while an animal undergoing brain surgery as part of an experiment wouldn't have any such consolation.

Some imaginative meat eaters tell themselves they can eat meat from factory farms without the animals suffering any harm at all. They believe that one person's decision to eat meat from an industrial farm won't make any difference. The supply chain is so long, their argument goes, with payments going from a consumer to a retailer to a distributor and then finally to the producer, that the producer won't even notice a single consumer's purchasing decision. As a result, they imagine it won't make any difference if they eat meat from a factory farm, because the same number of animals will still be raised there and slaughtered.[20]

While the intensive meat production system is massive and complex, its products are still subject to the economics of supply and demand.[21] As a result, one economist said, "[a]n individual changing their behavior will have exactly the long-run impact that they would expect—every chicken they choose not to buy will be one chicken somewhere down the supply chain in the future that does not die."[22]

* * *

Some meat producers have taken the denial that they harm animals to another level; they say they pamper the animals they raise. In 1997, Frank Perdue, the head of one of America's largest industrial producers, said his company's chickens "live in $60,000 houses, get eight hours of sleep and eat princely meals that include cookies for dessert," living a life he said was "chicken heaven." He said the sheds where the chickens lived were "spacious, specially constructed houses" where there is "no overcrowding" and "every bird has plenty of room to roam. To make friends, or find a quiet place of its own."[23,] Shown below is a photo of chickens being raised for Perdue's company that tells a different story, with hundreds of birds crammed together on the floor of a dark shed.[24]

A British producer used a different upscale metaphor. He said the chickens on their farm "live in a nice warm atmosphere out of the wind and rain, and have ad lib food. Rather like a club."[25]

Other producers say the animals on their farms aren't only willing to be used for food, they're happy to do it. One of the most well known is a campaign sponsored by the California Milk Advisory Board that said, "Great cheese comes from happy cows. Happy cows come from California." Ads in the campaign show cows contentedly grazing in lush pastures. Some include the slogan "So much grass, so little time." Making the task more manageable, though, the center of California's dairy industry is in the dry and barren Central Valley, where the cows are kept in dirt feedlots, not pastures.[26] Even if some cows were allowed to graze in pastures, though, they weren't likely to have been happy when their calves were taken from them shortly after being born and probably weren't happy when four or five years old and sent to slaughter after becoming sick or worn out from years of producing unnaturally high amounts of milk.

Following a similar strategy, the Happy Egg Company markets its eggs in the United Kingdom with photographs of hens happily "sunbathing" in a pasture. Like the California producers' claim that great cheese comes from happy cows, this company says in its advertisements that "happy eggs are wonderfully tasty," failing to mention the unhappy fate of male chicks who are killed soon after hatching because they're of no value to the company.[27]

Many meat eaters have ended up believing that current production methods effectively safeguard farmed animals' well-being, that "Meat is happy."[28] Some people even tell themselves that the animals are happy when they're slaughtered. A respondent in one study described the process this way: "[There's l]ike an assembly line, with splints to hold them, to apply pressure on the animals. . . . To apply pressure on an animal is almost like when we hug someone. . . .So animals feel relaxed when they are slaughtered."[29]

Some research scientists also claim that the animals they use are happy to help. They suggest that animals have volunteered to be part of their research team. One researcher spoke of dogs who had been subjected to chronic toxicity tests as "co-workers of ours."[30] Another, who inflicted brain damage on squirrel monkeys and cats in her experiments, referred to the animals she used as her "colleagues."[31]

Hunters tell themselves similar exonerative stories. Some have developed the Myth of the Willing Victim into a point of honor. Notwithstanding their use of camouflage, stealth, and deception while hunting, they believe that if a hunter has a pure heart and treats his prey with respect, they'll willingly give their life to him.[32] Rapists use similar myths to exonerate themselves from the harm they inflict.[33]

Farmers, research scientists, and hunters aren't the first people to claim that those they exploit are happy. Slaveholders perpetuated the Myth of the Happy Slave from antiquity until well into the nineteenth century.[34] Like the happiness of enslaved people, the happiness of animal victims is a fiction. The harms they suffer are real, though, whether hidden, hidden *from*, minimized, or denied altogether.

3

Denigrate the Victims

"They're Untermenschen *(subhuman)"*

"Self-censure for cruel conduct can be disengaged by stripping people of human qualities. Once dehumanized, they are no longer viewed as persons with feelings, hopes, and concerns but as subhuman objects."

—**Albert Bandura**, "Moral Disengagement in the Perpetration of Inhumanities," *Personality and Social Psychology Review* 3(3)(1999), 200.

Another way people avoid feeling guilty about harming others is to denigrate their victims. The Nazis did that when they claimed that the people they considered inferior were *Untermenschen*. When asked why they went to such great lengths to degrade people they were going to kill anyway, a death camp commandant explained that the victims had to be seen as subhuman beasts so that the men who operated the gas chambers would be less burdened by distress.[1]

As the Holocaust showed, divesting stigmatized people of human qualities can pave the way for genocide. Dehumanization makes them "less than human."[2] Once that happens, the moral rules that guide conduct between humans don't apply to them, and ordinary people can treat them in the most appalling ways with a clear conscience.[3]

As James Rachels noted in the quotation at the beginning of the introduction, if we think of other animals as sensitive and intelligent beings, the ways we exploit them may seem monstrous, so we resist thinking of them that way. If they don't have thoughts, feelings, and family bonds the same way we do, it may seem they're not fully alive. Just as dehumanization removes moral protection from members of disfavored human groups, devitalization strips animals of even the lesser protections we usually afford to them.

One way to devitalize animals is to see them as machine-like creatures incapable of suffering. This view can be traced back to René Descartes, a seventeenth-century philosopher and scientist. One of his contemporaries recalled that Cartesian scientists "administered beatings to dogs with perfect indifference, and made fun of those who pitied the creatures as if they felt pain. They said the animals were clocks; that the cries they emitted when struck were only the noise of a little spring that had been touched, but that the whole body was without feeling. They nailed poor animals up on boards by their four paws to vivisect them and see the circulation of blood, which was a great subject of conversation."[4] Most people now recognize that dogs are sentient creatures, not robotic automatons. And there's broad agreement among scientists that all other vertebrate animals can probably experience pain and suffer from it just as we do.[5]

Many scientists who use animals in experiments, however, continue to treat them as objects, commonly referring to male or female animals as *it*. When researchers failed to do that in manuscripts they submitted, editors at the *Journal of Experimental Medicine* used to substitute *it* for *he* or *she* in articles they published.[6] Researchers commonly number, batch, and discard animals as if they're supplies, not sentient creatures. Recalling days when research programs could purchase a monkey for only twenty-five dollars, a veterinary researcher commented "You'd use one once and you'd throw it away."[7] Objectifying the animals they use, may help researchers assuage any guilt they feel. A woman who conducted invasive experiments on female rabbits said, "I find it's easier to think of them as test tubes, rather than animals—warm, furry test tubes."[8]

In 1988, the objectification of animals used by research scientists reached a new point legally when the United States Patent and Trademark Office issued a patent on mice genetically modified with an active cancer gene.[9] This was a new point morally, too. For the first time, a nation granted a property interest in animals intentionally designed to suffer.[10]

Meat producers objectify the animals they raise, too. They use manufacturing terms like *converting machines* or *production units* when referring to them. A representative of a meat company advised pork producers that "[t]he breeding sow should be thought of, and treated as, a valuable piece of machinery whose function is to pump out baby pigs like a sausage machine."[11] One pork producer advised others to "[f]orget the pig is an animal. Treat him just like a machine in a factory. Schedule treatments like you would lubrication. Breeding season like the first step in an assembly line. And marketing like the delivery of finished goods."[12] Although meat producers adopt the jargon and processes of manufacturers, their "products" differ from manufactured products in a morally significant way: they're sentient creatures with intrinsic worth and ties to other sentient creatures.[13] The belief that other animals aren't sentient is a legitimizing myth people use to feel better about exploiting them.[14]

* * *

Depersonalization is another way to reduce the moral status of disfavored groups. As one Holocaust scholar recounted:

> The Germans almost never took pains to learn the names of a camp's inmates; in Auschwitz, they denied the very existence of a person's name—this mark of humanity—tattooing each with a number which, with the exception of some privileged prisoners, was the only identifying label used by the camp's staff. In Auschwitz, there were no Mosches, Ivans, or Lechs, but only prisoners with numbers like 10431 or 69771. . . . [D]ehumanizing each person by robbing him of his individuality, by rendering each, to the German eye, but another body in an undifferentiated mass, was but the first step towards fashioning their "subhumans."[15]

Giving someone a name recognizes their uniqueness; referring to them with a number does just the opposite.[16] That may be why research scientists who use animals identify them with numbers, not names,[17] a standard practice for decades. In the 1930s, a co-editor of the *Journal of Experimental Medicine* directed those submitting articles for potential publication to "never use names."[18] When we give animals names, they become personified and we're under considerable pressure to treat them as *persons.*[19] The chief technician in one laboratory had to tell a worker to stop naming the sheep they used because that made it harder for others to perform experiments on them.[20]

Meat producers usually don't give names to the animals they raise, either. Sometimes, though, they're inclined to name some animals they've gotten to know. Two pork producers warned other producers to "resist the temptation to become too attached. If you're going to eat it, don't give it a pet name. Try something like 'Porky' or 'Chops' or 'Spare-ribs' if the urge to name is too strong."[21]

* * *

As Gordon Allport noted in his seminal book about prejudice, categorization helps us make sense of the world.[22] It can lead us astray, though, when we divide people into categories and make judgments about them based on the category in which we've put them.[23]

This can happen with animals, too. The category of *food animals* is a good example. In one study, psychologists investigated whether people considered animals less able to suffer if they were categorized as food. They asked eighty Americans to evaluate whether tree kangaroos were sentient and deserved moral respect. They told them either that the kangaroos were considered food by people living in Papua New Guinea or simply that the kangaroos lived there. People who were told that the kangaroos were food animals judged them to be less capable of suffering and less deserving of moral concern than those who weren't told that.[24] It was much the same in other studies.[25]

Many people enjoy eating meat but think it's wrong to harm sentient creatures, creating a moral conflict called the *meat paradox*.[26] One way people resolve the meat paradox is to tell themselves that the animals they eat aren't sentient or intelligent. The authors of one study summarized their findings this way: "In the abstract, when presented with foreign or fictitious animals eaten by distant or nonexistent people, we see intelligent animals as worthy of our moral concern. When these animals are closer to home and we are the eaters, intelligence becomes conveniently irrelevant. Smart animals deserve our moral concern, unless, of course, we want to eat them."[27]

A similar moral paradox confronts those who conduct animal research: they don't want to harm sentient animals yet perform experiments that do just that. Some researchers resolve the conflict with categorization, telling themselves that the animals are just *laboratory animals* bred to be used in research.

Whether the animals are categorized as *food animals* or *laboratory animals*, they fit into the larger demeaning category of *animals*. In a classic experiment, Albert Bandura and some colleagues told a group of college students they were going to train another group of students from a nearby college. They divided the "trainers" into three groups and allowed each group to overhear an assistant characterize the group to be trained as either "nice," "like animals," or in neutral terms. The researchers gave the "trainers" authority to "punish" members of the other group for deficient performance with sham electric shocks of varying intensity. The students "shocked" those said to be "like animals" the most severely.[28] In a comment about the experiment, a colleague of Bandura's wrote "Thus, a single word—*animals*—was sufficient to incite intelligent college students to treat those so labeled as if they deserved to be harmed."[29]

≈ 4 ≈

Disparage the Critics

"The Abolitionists Are Hypocrites"

"Derogation of those working toward ecological preservation is a common tactic for neutralising moral concern over lifestyle practices that impair the ecological supports of life. The proponents are disparaged as '*doomsayers*,' '*scaremongers*,' '*environmental wackos*,' '*tree huggers*,' and the like."

—**Albert Bandura**, "Impeding Ecological Sustainability Through Selective Moral Disengagement," *International Journal of Innovation and Sustainable Development* 2(1)(2009), 22.

People who are criticized sometimes respond by disparaging their critics instead of responding to their arguments. Southern slaveholders in the United States did that when they said that abolitionists from England and the North were in no position to pass judgment upon them. While they might not be slave owners any longer, the Southerners said, British and Northern slave merchants had kidnapped and sold most of the Africans enslaved in the South. As one put it, "To New-England and Old England, the South almost wholly owes her slaves. They stole the African from his native land, and bartered him away, without a care (about) what became of him afterwards; their philanthropy by no means disquieted at the reflection that he might fall into the hands of those who might brutally entreat him . . ."[1]

In his classic defense of animal experimentation, Carl Cohen also charged critics with hypocrisy, writing that:

> [o]ne cannot coherently object to the killing of animals in biomedical investigations while continuing to eat them. . . . the consistent objector must not only refrain from all eating of animals but also protest as vehemently against others eating them as well as others experimenting upon them. No less vigorously must the critic object to the wearing of animal hides in coats and shoes, to employment in any industrial enterprise that uses animal parts, and to any commercial development that will cause death or distress to animals.[2]

Vegetarians often elicit similar charges of hypocrisy from meat eaters who challenge them with questions like "Aren't plants alive, too?", "Do you feed meat to your pets?" and "Do you wear leather?"[3] Anthony Bourdain, a celebrity chef, was especially harsh in his criticism, saying "Vegetarians and the Hezbollah-like splinter faction, the vegans, are a persistent irritant to any chef worth a damn. . . . Vegetarians are the enemy of everything good and decent in the human spirit, an affront to all I stand for, the pure enjoyment of food."[4]

People who eat meat commonly view the dietary decisions of those who don't as criticism[5] and respond in kind. They tend to see men who follow a plant-based diet as less than fully masculine, putting them in the same devalued group as women.[6] Men and women who don't consume animal products for ethical reasons are devalued the most.[7] In one study, American respondents evaluated vegetarians and vegans more negatively than Black people. Of all the disfavored groups included in that survey, only drug addicts were rated more negatively than vegetarians and vegans.[8]

Disparaging those who criticize the exploitation of animals has a long history. In his monumental treatise on ethics, the seventeenth-century Dutch philosopher Benedict de Spinoza wrote that "the law against killing animals is based on an empty superstition and womanish tenderness, rather than upon sound reason."[9]

As Spinoza's remarks suggest, gender-based disparagement of those who oppose animal exploitation has a long history, too. When women opposed vivisection in the nineteenth century, they were dismissed as being overly emotional. When men opposed it, they were said to be "effeminate," a code word for the sexist stereotype that women are sentimental and irrational.[10] Similar disparaging stereotypes continue to the present day. In a 2010 interview, a Swedish researcher described vivisection opponents as "confused girls."[11]

Another scientist—who conducted head transplant research on rhesus monkeys—said that people who were concerned about the suffering of animals used in research were either prejudiced against science or mentally ill, writing:

> I am simply unable to plumb the depths of a philosophy that places such a premium on animal life even at the expense of human existence and improvement. It would appear that this preoccupation with the alleged pain and suffering of the animals used in medical research may well represent, at the very least, social prejudice against medicine or, more seriously, true psychiatric aberrations.[12]

This was reminiscent of some vivisectionists' earlier claim that their opponents were animal lovers who suffered from a form of madness they called "zoophil-psychosis."[13]

In the 1990s, some researchers began a campaign to educate the public about the need to use animals in scientific research. Moral reversal was a central part of the campaign. They denied that their experiments were inhumane, saying their critics were the ones acting inhumanely by working to stop research that would save lives and prevent much human suffering.[14] One wrote:

> The animal rights movement illustrates the incoherent nature of a moral passion become immoral by virtue of its extremism. In the name of this laudable quality of humaneness, the use of animals for food, clothing, and medical experimentation is prohibited. Research that could save your child's life, or save you from an excruciating disease, is declared unethical. The result is inhumanity towards man.[15]

When researchers claim that their critics are inhumane, it's like the pot calling the kettle black. It doesn't make the pot any less black or animal research any less inhumane.

5

Displace Responsibility

Adolph Eichmann: "Like Pontius Pilate, I felt free of guilt"

"[People] are spared self-disapproving reactions by shifting the responsibility to others or to situational circumstances. This absolves them of personal responsibility for the harm they are causing."

—**Albert Bandura**, "Impeding Ecological Sustainability Through Selective Moral Disengagement," *International Journal of Innovation and Sustainable Development* 2(1)(2007), 19.

After he was captured and brought to trial in Israel, Adolf Eichmann took the witness stand in his own defense. Speaking about the 1942 conference in which senior Nazis discussed their plan to exterminate eleven million European Jews, he said, "I felt something of the satisfaction of Pilate, because I felt entirely innocent of any guilt. The leading figures of the Reich at the time had spoken at the Wannsee Conference, the 'Popes' had given their orders; it was up to me to obey, and that is what I bore in mind over the future years."[1]

When he claimed others were responsible for the harm he helped cause, Eichmann was using the simplest method of moral disengagement: blaming someone else for it. If people like him cause harm while acting as part of a group, they can displace responsibility to senior members of their group, as he did, by claiming that they were just following orders.

People can also evade responsibility by blaming someone from a different group. Consumers and producers often blame each other for the harm animals suffer when raised on a factory farm. Consumers say farmers are at fault for using methods of production that cause the animals to suffer great harm.[2] Producers respond by saying they have to use cost-efficient industrial methods because consumers aren't willing to pay the higher cost of more animal-friendly methods of production.[3]

Another way people try to avoid responsibility for harming others is to claim they didn't cause the harm willingly, that they had no choice. One of the most common justifications people give for eating meat is to say they have to eat meat to be healthy. They believe they can't get the protein and other nutrients their body needs without eating at least some meat.[4] At one time, many dieticians believed that, too. Not anymore. Beginning in the 1980s, after large-scale studies showed that vegetarians were less likely to suffer from some chronic diseases and tended to live longer, nutrition experts began viewing well-balanced vegetarian diets as a healthy alternative to meat-based ones.[5] As the American Dietetic Association put it in a 2009 paper, "... appropriately planned vegetarian diets, including total vegetarian or vegan diets, are healthful, nutritionally adequate, and may provide health benefits in the prevention and treatment of certain diseases."[6]

Omnivores use another form of the "I have no choice" displacement when they claim that humans are natural carnivores. It isn't our fault that we've been shaped by evolution to crave meat, they say, it's just part of nature. They may also justify eating meat by pointing out that some animals eat other animals and we're animals, so it isn't wrong for us to do that, too. As mentioned earlier, in *The Omnivore's Dilemma*, Michael Pollan dismissed the idea that we should base our moral decisions on what's natural, noting that murder and rape occur in the natural world.[7]

Nature and Morality

The fact that humans have survived by dominating other species does not in itself show that we are morally justified in continuing to act in the same way. Humans have evolved a capacity to reflect upon their own behavior. Much of this reflection has taken place by means of civilization and especially education, which have channeled and changed 'natural' behavior. Attitudes toward many forms of behavior once justified as natural, as, for example, the dominance of men over women, or the keeping of slaves, have changed substantially in a great number of societies (reference omitted).

The Ethics of Research Involving Animals: The Report of the Nuffield Council on Bioethics (London: Nuffield Council on Bioethics, 2005), 40.

Scientists who conduct animal research also say they have no choice; they must use animals because there aren't any morally acceptable alternatives. Carl Cohen made the case this way in his defense of animal experimentation:

Every advance in medicine—every new drug, new operation, new therapy of any kind—must sooner or later be tried on a living being for the first time.... The subject of that experiment, if it is not an animal, will be a human being. Prohibiting the use of live animals in biomedical research, therefore, or sharply restricting it, must result either in the blockage of much valuable research or in the replacement of animal subjects with human subjects.[8]

Whether perpetrators blame someone or something else for their transgressions, they could have refused to harm anyone, no matter how strong the pressure was from others or from the situation that they were in. In the end, we're responsible for what we do, no matter what we tell other people. Or ourselves.

≈ 6 ≈

Diffuse Responsibility

Nazi Doctor at Auschwitz:
"I am a victim of the environment, no less than the inmates"

"When everyone is responsible, no one really feels responsible."

—**Albert Bandura**, *Moral Disengagement: How People Do Harm and Live with Themselves* (New York: Worth Publishers, 2016), 62.

Instead of shifting responsibility to *someone*, perpetrators sometimes blame *everyone*. A doctor at Auschwitz who selected which newly arrived prisoners would be sent directly to a gas chamber and killed others with lethal injections could tell himself, "*I* am not responsible for selections. *I* am not responsible for phenol injections. *I* am a victim of the environment no less than the inmates."[1] As Atticus Finch told his daughter in the movie *To Kill a Mockingbird,* "A mob is a place where people go to take a break from their conscience."

People commonly justify eating meat by saying that almost everyone does it,[2] suggesting that behavior so widespread can't be wrong. Even if people all over the world have done something for a long time, that hasn't made it right.[3] Slavery is as old as civilization and was practiced all over the world.[4] Men used their power to dominate and exploit women for centuries. That didn't make either slavery or the subordination of women right.

In a variation of the "it's normal" rationalization, some people justify experiments that use animals by pointing to the acceptability of many other exploitative ways people treat animals. Carl Cohen did that when he argued:

> Killing animals to meet human needs for food, clothing, and shelter is judged entirely reasonable by most persons. The ubiquity of these uses and the virtual universality of moral support for them confront the opponent of research using animals with an inescapable difficulty. How can the many common uses of animals be judged morally worthy, while their use in scientific investigation is judged unworthy?[5]

Another way people diffuse responsibility is to say that although they may have harmed someone, what they did was entirely legal. One proponent of animal research even argued:

> . . . *animals actually enjoy greater protection* than do human subjects since, unlike federal regulations over human experimentation, (the United States) Animal Welfare Act applies *whether or not federal funding supports the experiment* (italics in original). Moreover, experiments using people are not subject to surprise government inspections but must rely exclusively on institutional review boards (IRBs) for oversight. Further, there is no government agency equivalent to the Animal and Plant Health Inspection Service to protect human subjects, no matter how vulnerable or defenseless the people being experimented upon may be, nor is there an organization that provides inspection and accreditation services equivalent to the AAALAC.[6]

In fact, the Animal Welfare Act only requires that food, water, and shelter be provided to some animals used in research unless the experiment requires otherwise. And it provides no protection to rats and mice bred for research, the animals used most often in experiments.

Along the same lines, laws often fail to protect farmed animals from cruel treatment. Just as the Animal Welfare Act fails to cover most of the animals used in research, it doesn't provide any protection to animals used on farms. The same is true of many states' animal cruelty laws, which include exemptions for any treatment of farmed animals that's "accepted," "common," or "customary."[7] In these states, it's against the law to engage in animal cruelty unless it's a normal farming practice. Then it's legal.

What happened in Iowa is a good example of how the laws thought to protect animals often don't. As mentioned earlier, in 2020 a meat producer there roasted alive more than 200,000 pigs and piglets by sealing the barns where they were confined, shutting off ventilation, and turning up the heat. Under the state's animal cruelty laws, "A person is guilty of animal torture if the person intentionally or knowingly inflicts on an animal severe and prolonged or repeated physical pain that causes the animal's serious injury or death."[8] While the producer's conduct appears to qualify as animal torture, Iowa's animal cruelty laws don't provide any protection to pigs or other animals commonly raised for food.[9]

∼ 7 ∼

The Exonerative Use of Comparisons

"At least we didn't kill any children."

> "How behavior is viewed is colored by what it is compared against. By exploiting the contrast principle, reprehensible acts can be made righteous."
>
> —**Albert Bandura**, "Moral Disengagement in the Perpetration of Inhumanities," *Personality and Social Psychology Review* 3(3)(1999), 195–196.

Some of the German police who massacred Polish Jews during World War II considered killing children abhorrent and shied away from doing it. During a postwar trial, one defended his unit's involvement in the massacres, saying that "among the Jews shot in our section of town, there were no infants or small children. I would like to say that almost tacitly everyone refrained from shooting infants and small children."[1]

When they use the "at least it isn't as bad as that" method of moral disengagement, people try to put their behavior in a more positive light by contrasting it with other conduct that seems worse. Many of those who harm animals do that by comparing the harm they cause to the suffering of animals on industrial farms, as one hunter did when he said, "... my venison was happy and free until the moment of its death while my chicken was probably cooped up its whole life."[2] Less intensive meat producers also use factory farms as the disfavored contrast when they promote their products as *cage-free*, *free-range*, *grass-fed*, or *pasture-raised*.

Making their own disfavored contrast, factory farm operators claim that the animals they raise enjoy a safer and healthier life than they would in the wild. They say they protect animals on their farms from predators, disease, and bad weather while providing them with nutritious food, veterinary care, and a quick death.[3]

Scientists who conduct experiments on animals also compare the harm they inflict to that caused by meat producers. Carl Cohen did that when he argued that "[a]nesthetics and thoughtful animal husbandry render the level of actual animal distress in the laboratory generally lower than that in the abattoir."[4] In another exonerative comparison, he said that the number of dogs and cats killed in experiments at the time was "less than one-fiftieth of the number of dogs and cats killed *in animal shelters by humane societies for convenience,* because we have no place for them."[5]

A more subtle form of exonerative comparison is to adopt language from a benign activity to make an injurious one seem less harmful.[6] As discussed earlier, meat producers do that when they borrow a term from plant-based farming—a less morally troubling practice—by calling their industry *animal agriculture* and saying they *harvest* the animals.

Pork producers have come up with their own benign comparisons. An industry textbook called the crates where pregnant sows are confined—so small the pig can't even turn around—an "individual accommodation."[7, 8] After a sow has given birth, intensive hog farm operators tether her in another small crate that one producer said was a "modern maternity unit."[9] And after producers take piglets from their mothers and cram them with other piglets in a windowless industrial shed, they say the piglets are in a "nursery."[10]

⁓ 8 ⁌

Moral Justification

"Shooting the children soothed my conscience."

"... given people's dexterous facility for justifying violent means, all kinds of inhumanities get clothed in moral wrappings."

—**Albert Bandura**, "Moral Disengagement in the Perpetration of Inhumanities," *Personality and Social Psychology Review* 3(3)(1999), 195.

Not content to use exonerative comparisons to make the harm they cause seem less blameworthy, some perpetrators say that what they've done isn't blameworthy at all because they did it for an honorable reason. One of them, a German police officer who specialized in killing children during massacres of Polish Jews, said it soothed his conscience to think he had saved the children from the suffering they would certainly have endured after other officers had killed their mothers.[1]

As Bandura pointed out, people who use moral justification to justify wrongful behavior can cause even more harm than those who use other methods of disengagement because believing that it's justified can lead them to become more efficient at harming others and even take pride in doing it.[2] Carl Cohen is a case in point. Responding to those who said humane values require using fewer animals in research when possible, he countered, "Should we not at least reduce the use of animals in biomedical research? No, we should increase it, to avoid when feasible the use of humans as experimental subjects."[3, 4] To protect humans, he said, we're morally obliged to pursue "the wide and imaginative use of live animal subjects...."[5]

According to Cohen, animal experimentation is morally justified from a utilitarian point of view because the human suffering it prevents far outweighs the suffering of the animals used. As he put it:

> Critics relying (however mistakenly) on animal rights may claim to ignore the beneficial results of such research, rights being trump cards to which interest and advantage must give way. But an argument that is explicitly framed in terms of interest and benefit for all over the long run must attend also to the disadvantageous consequences of not using animals in research, and to all the achievements attained and attainable only through their use. The sum of the benefits of their use is utterly beyond quantification. The elimination of horrible disease, the increase of longevity, the avoidance of great pain, the saving of lives, and the improvement of the quality of lives (for humans and for animals) achieved through research using animals is so incalculably great that the argument of these critics, systematically pursued, establishes not their conclusion but its reverse: to refrain from using animals in biomedical research is, on utilitarian grounds, morally wrong.[6]

Cohen didn't attempt to quantify the benefits that are derived from experiments on animals, calling them "utterly beyond quantification" and "incalculably great." Completing a valid utilitarian analysis, however, requires comparing benefits to costs, and to do that the benefits must be measured somehow. In addition, Cohen's assessment of the benefits is incomplete; any benefits must be reduced by the costs that humans suffer from ineffective or harmful treatments prompted by animal research and the loss of effective treatments that flunked animal testing and weren't developed.[7] In addition, valid assessments don't include benefits from discoveries that would have been made without experimenting on animals.

Even the enormous benefits Cohen attributed to animal experimentation don't justify the experiments if they're morally repugnant. Nazi researchers soaked Jewish prisoners in cold water and placed them in refrigerators to learn how hypothermia develops and how it can be treated. Although Cohen thought much valuable information had been discovered from these experiments, he said that morality forbids us from advancing medicine through immoral means, no matter how great the benefits.[8]

Predicting the benefits that will result from any research project is unavoidably speculative. Assessing the harm that animals suffer is just as problematic. Their well-being can't be measured with any precision. In addition, the criteria commonly used to assess their welfare are critically deficient. They only measure the harm that animals suffer while being experimented upon, failing to take into account the distress they suffer before that, including the fear and anxiety they experience while being captured, handled, and transported.[9] They also fail to consider the loss of autonomy they suffer from being confined.[10] Loss of freedom can be an extremely significant harm; one of the most common ways we punish people for serious transgressions is to confine them.

These criteria also fail to consider the harm that animals suffer when they're killed. As mentioned in the chapter about the exonerative use of language, researchers often use words like *sacrifice*, *dispatch*, or *terminate* when they refer to killing the animals they've used in experiments. They may do this because most people understand that death negatively affects an animal's welfare. When a veterinary ethicist asked audiences if they thought the painless killing of rhesus monkeys used in an experiment negatively affected their welfare, many people laughed at his question. When he asked why they were laughing, they said it was obvious that the monkeys' welfare was negatively affected by being killed.[11] They were right. Killing healthy, sentient animals harms them by depriving them of pleasurable experiences they may have enjoyed in the future.[12] Nevertheless, most contemporary methods of assessment fail to recognize that killing animals used in research causes them harm (except when the research has so compromised their welfare that death comes as a relief to them).[13]

The great difficulty of assessing the costs and benefits of animal experimentation and the deficiencies of contemporary assessments make any utilitarian calculations extremely unreliable. In the United States, most institutions that engage in animal research use an Institutional Care and Use Committee (ICAUC) to decide whether to approve a proposed research project. A 2001 study compared the decisions of 50 ICAUCs to those that a different committee had reached regarding the same project. The second committee agreed with the first committee's decision less than a quarter of the time.[14] One commentator wrote that this method of deciding whether to approve a research project was no more reliable than flipping a coin.[15]

* * *

People who defend industrial meat production sometimes justify it by using a similar cost-benefit argument; they say the cost efficiencies of industrial production allow it to feed the world, a human benefit that far outweighs the harm animals suffer. One put it this way: "Access to nutritional, inexpensive food is a great benefit to people on limited budgets. Thus, although CAFOs[16] clearly do not provide animals with an optimal environment, they do promote a substantial human good by bringing affordable meat to hundreds of millions of people."[17] Defenders of slavery once offered a similar justification, claiming that it clothed the world by enabling the poor to buy inexpensive clothing.[18]

Actually, animal agriculture isn't efficient; it's enormously wasteful. Depending on the type of meat produced and the method of production, it takes 6–17 times more land, 4.4–26 times more water, and 6–20 times more fossil fuel to produce a gram of protein from animals than it does to produce one from soy.[19] It's such a wasteful way to make food that animal agriculture uses about eighty-three percent of the world's farmland but provides only thirty-seven percent of the protein in our diets and eighteen percent of the calories.[20] Some of this inefficiency comes from the way meat is produced. About forty percent of worldwide grain production is fed to animals.[21] Feeding grain to animals and then eating the animals wastes ninety percent of the grain's protein and ninety-six percent of its calories.[22]

Meanwhile, more than 700 million people are undernourished.[23] Half of the grain fed to livestock would be more than enough to feed all of them.[24] Not only are the grain and soy that are fed to animals unavailable for hungry people to eat, but using them to produce meat also creates demand that drives up the price of that which remains available. Impoverished people suffer the most from this because they can't afford the higher prices.[25] Even with industrial meat production's cost efficiencies, meat remains a luxury people living in food-insecure parts of the world often can't afford. A 2012 study found that a meat-based diet in urban India costs 10 percent more than a vegetarian diet and 13.8 percent more than a vegan one.[26]

Factory farms, then, don't feed the world. As Jonathan Safran Foer wrote in *We Are the Weather,* they starve it.[27]

* * *

Like many who use moral justification to exonerate themselves for harming others, Carl Cohen didn't shy away from the ethical issues raised by animal experimentation; he addressed them head-on. Responding to critics who said that treating humans better than other animals is *speciesism*, he defended the better treatment people receive, saying, "I am a speciesist. Speciesism is not merely plausible; it is essential for right conduct, because those who will not make the morally relevant distinctions among species are almost certain, in consequence, to misapprehend their true obligations."[28]

While defending speciesism, Cohen was quick to condemn racism and sexism, commenting, "Racists, even if acting on the basis of mistaken factual beliefs, do grave moral wrong precisely because there is no morally relevant distinction among the races. The supposition of such differences has led to outright horror. The same is true of the sexes, neither being entitled by right to greater respect or concern than the other."[29] For him, though, speciesism isn't as wrong as racism or sexism because there's a morally relevant difference between humans and all other animals. He claimed that the animals deserve to have a lower moral status because they don't have a sense of morality and can't be members of a group who act morally toward each other.[30] For example, he said, "Humans engage in moral reflection, while rats are somewhat foreign to that enterprise."[31]

Ironically, experiments conducted by animal researchers showed that rats can act empathically,[32] the root of altruism[33] and morality[34] in humans.[35] In one experiment, rats quickly learned how to free another rat trapped in a plexiglass container inside their cage. When a second container with chocolate chips was placed in their cage, the rats could open it and eat all the chocolate themselves before freeing the other rat. Still, over half of them shared the chocolate with the rat they freed. As with humans, some rats acted more empathically than others, and the females tended to act more empathically than the males.[36]

Another experiment also involved a rat trapped in a plexiglass container. This time, though, after some rats had learned to cross a dry area and free the trapped rat, researchers added a pool of water in the dry area. Although rats experience distress when in the water, most of the rats swam or jumped across the water to free another rat. The authors concluded that these rats acted altruistically by putting themselves in distress to help another rat without expecting to receive a reward of any kind.[37, 38]

Other experiments have shown that mice—another group of rodents frequently experimented upon by research scientists—also engage in pro-social behavior and have the capacity for empathy. In a 2006 experiment, mice responded with intensified pain responses when they saw other mice in pain,[39] a behavior the primatologist Frans de Waal referred to as "the oldest kind of empathy."[40]

Decades before studies found empathic behavior in rats and mice, other studies showed that rhesus monkeys—animals commonly used in several types of research—can act altruistically. In a series of experiments conducted in the 1960s, researchers wanted to see if monkeys who learned to pull a chain to get food pellets would still do that after they saw that pulling it also gave an electric shock to a monkey in an adjacent compartment. They found that most of the monkeys would refuse to pull the chain if it meant that another monkey would get shocked.[41] One monkey stopped pulling the chain for five days and a second one for twelve days, starving themselves to avoid hurting another monkey.[42]

Empathic behavior has also been found in several other species, including chimpanzees, elephants, and dolphins.[43] It's so common that authors of a recent review said, "Since empathy behaviors have been observed in species ranging from mice to elephants, the debate should no longer be about whether animals have empathy; instead, what are the mechanisms that engage it."[44]

Of course, these studies don't show that other animals have moral systems as complex as our own. However, there are different kinds and degrees of moral agency, and the belief that only humans have a sense of morality is mistaken.[45] Morality likely evolved in social animals, and the difference between our moral behavior and theirs is, as Charles Darwin suggested, a difference in degree, not a difference in kind.[46] Commenting on the evolutionary basis of human morality, Frans de Waal wrote:

> To neglect the common ground with other primates, and to deny the evolutionary roots of human morality, would be like arriving at the top of a tower to declare that the rest of the building is irrelevant, that the precious concept of "tower" ought to be reserved for the summit. While making for good academic fights, semantics are mostly a waste of time. Are animals moral? Let us simply conclude that they occupy several floors of the tower of morality. Rejection of even this modest proposal can only result in an impoverished view of the structure as a whole.[47]

* * *

Carl Cohen wasn't the first person to believe that humans are different from and superior to all other animals. Beliefs in human supremacy go back millennia. Thinking of ourselves as different from all the other members of the animal kingdom made it easier for us to harm them in ways that would be wrong if done to other

The Moral Principle of Equality

We learn from Darwin that, contrary to what was previously believed, humans and other animals are not radically different in kind; and with this new understanding we are compelled to reason differently:

> Individuals are to be treated in the same way, unless there is a difference between them that justifies a difference in treatment.
>
> Humans and other animals are not radically different in kind; they are similar in some ways, and different in others, and these differences are often merely matters of degree. If humans are rational, so are other animals, although perhaps to a different degree. The same goes for other important human capacities.
>
> Therefore, when humans have characteristics that justify treating them in certain ways, it may be that other animals also have these characteristics.
>
> Therefore, our treatment of humans and other animals should be sensitive to the pattern of similarities and differences that exist between them. When there is a difference that justifies treating them differently, we may, but when there is no such difference, we may not.

James Rachels, *Created from Animals: The Moral Implications of Darwinism* (Oxford: Oxford University Press, 1990), 197.

humans. According to the Welsh historian Keith Thomas: "In drawing a firm line between man and beast, the main purpose of early modern theorists was to justify hunting, domestication, meat-eating, vivisection (which became common scientific practice in the late seventeenth century) and the wholesale extermination of vermin and predators."[48]

One of those early modern theorists, René Descartes, also believed that people could use the human-animal divide to exonerate themselves for harming animals, writing that the unbridgeable gulf he drew between humans and other animals was "not so much cruel to wild beasts as favorable to men, whom it absolves... of any suspicion of crime, however often they may eat or kill animals."[49]

As the moral philosopher James Rachels noted in the introductory quotation at the beginning of the book, many of the ways we treat animals would be monstrous if done to other people, compelling us to come up with justifications for treating animals differently. The rationales have changed with the times. In Thomas Aquinas' day, when moral status was based on having a soul, that was what animals lacked. When the capacity to reason became determinative in the Cartesian world, that was what they lacked.[50]

Now that we've learned more about other animals, we realize that all the characteristics we thought made us unique are actually shared by some other animals. As de Waal noted, we now know that instead of a gap between the cognition of humans and other animals, there's "a gently sloping beach created by the steady pounding of millions of waves. Even if human intellect is higher up on the beach, it was shaped by the same forces battering the same shore."[51] If we're higher up on the shore and have a wider range of mental capacities, that still doesn't entitle us to a special moral status in the animal kingdom, any more than brilliant people deserve special treatment in the human world.[52] And even if our intelligence is superior to theirs, that doesn't give us the right to dominate and exploit them.[53]

All candidates for human exceptionalism have gone through a similar life cycle.[54] According to de Waal, claims of human uniqueness "typically cycle through four stages: they are repeated over and over, they are challenged by new findings, they hobble toward retirement, and then they are dumped in an ignominious grave."[55] That has been the fate of language, culture, morality, and all the others.[56] Nevertheless, some people stubbornly point to one difference or another to justify the many ways we harm and exploit other animals, prompting one moral philosopher to satirize their reasoning this way:

> Since he has no language, he may be killed to make a tasty dish. Since she lacks the capacity to abstract and conceive the future, she may be hunted and killed for amusement. Since they are not capable of forming goals by considering alternatives, they may be used in lethal experiments. Since he lacks an epistemic relation to his interest in life, he may be killed in order that his body may be used for making soap and perfume. Since she lacks a cultural life, she may be trapped and skinned to make a fur coat.[57]

The Interconnection of Prejudices Against People and Animals

"Those who support animal exploitation also tend to endorse sexist and racist views and rely on the belief in group dominance and human supremacy to justify systems of inequality and oppression. The common denominator is that the interests of disadvantaged groups like animals, women, and ethnic minorities, are considered subordinate to the interests and privileges of advantaged groups like humans in general, and white men in particular."

—**Kristof Dhont et al.**, "The Psychology of Speciesism," in *Why We Love and Exploit Animals: Bridging Insights from Academia and Advocacy*, edited by Kristof Dhont and Gordon Hodson (New York: Routledge, 2020), 29.

By now, you may have noticed that people who exploit other animals use the same methods to feel better about it as those who once exploited other people. Today's meat producers and research scientists consider the animals they use to be inanimate machinery in much the same way that nineteenth-century slave owners thought of the people they enslaved. Meat eaters justify their diet as natural and necessary in the same way defenders of slavery once justified their "peculiar institution."[1] People who exploit animals say their victims aren't very intelligent or don't really feel pain, just as those who exploited other people did.[2] Exploiters of animals and people both hide the harm they inflict with euphemisms and innocuous-sounding language. And both respond to those who accuse them of hypocrisy by claiming that their critics are hypocrites themselves.

This isn't just a coincidence. As Gordon Allport famously noted in his 1954 classic, *The Nature of Prejudice*, "[i]f a person is anti-Jewish, he is likely to be anti-Catholic, anti-Negro, anti any out-group."[3] Subsequent research has confirmed Allport's impression, finding that those with negative attitudes about one disfavored group of people are more likely to be prejudiced against other disfavored groups as well, a correlation known as *generalized prejudice*.[4] Early studies found that people who were prejudiced against ethnic minorities were more likely to be prejudiced against members of racial minorities, too.[5] Later research showed that racists were more likely to be sexists as well.[6] More recent research has found that someone who supports the dominance of an elite group of people is more likely to endorse the exploitation of animals for human benefit.[7] Other recent studies have shown that the supremacists' penchant for domination often extends to the natural world, leading them to favor exploiting the environment in unsustainable ways.[8] These studies have effectively updated Allport's insight about the generalization of prejudice to become: "If a person is anti-Jewish, he is likely to be anti-Catholic, anti-Negro, anti-women, anti-animal, and anti-environment."[9, 10]

At first glance, the notion that some people are prejudiced against animals may seem odd.[11] Until recently, our understanding of prejudice applied only to relationships between people. Evidence has accrued from diverse sources, however, that racists and sexists have much in common with human supremacists:[12, 13]

- Often they're the same people; racists and sexists frequently have negative attitudes and beliefs about animals, too.[14]
- Racists, sexists, and believers in human supremacy are all more likely to support systems of group-based dominance and social inequality.[15]
- They all act in similar ways to members of groups they dominate, oppressing and exploiting them.[16]
- They all use similar myths and stereotypes about disfavored groups to legitimize oppressing and exploiting them, as discussed in the previous chapters.
- Like the negative attitudes and beliefs that underlie racism and sexism, ideological beliefs in human supremacy tend to be stable over time.[17]
- Like racists and sexists, believers in human supremacy tend to be lower in empathy than other people[18]
- Racists, sexists, and human supremacists are all more likely to support the exploitation of the natural world.[19]

Recently, a group of psychologists at the University of Oxford set out to determine the extent to which human supremacism can be considered a form of prejudice by testing whether believers in human supremacy tend to be prejudiced against disfavored groups of people, too, and whether human supremacism is driven by the same factors as prejudices against human groups. After conducting five studies that showed that it was significantly related to racism, sexism, and homophobia, they concluded that human supremacism "can be considered a psychological prejudice analogous to other forms of prejudice."[20]

The insults prejudiced people hurl at those they demean often show the connection between ethnic prejudice and human supremacism. According to a Palestinian nursery rhyme, "Palestine is our country. The Jews our dogs." Some Israelis feel much the same way about Palestinians. In 2000 a rabbi commented in an Israeli newspaper that "Arabs are the same as animals. There is no animal worse than them."[21] Comparing someone to an animal would lose its sting, of course, if animals weren't seen as inferior.[22] Because they are, the denigration of animals provides a model for prejudice against human groups.[23] Comparing stigmatized people to animals dehumanizes them and moves them from the elevated moral status we give humans to a lower level where we place animals.

While nonhuman animals can't be dehumanized, people can deprive them of moral consideration by denying that they're intelligent or able to suffer, a method of devaluation known as *dementalization*.[24] A study mentioned earlier is a good example. In that study, some people were told that tree kangaroos were considered food animals by people living in New Guinea, while others were just told that the kangaroos lived in New Guinea. Those who were told that the kangaroos were food animals judged them to be less capable of suffering and less worthy of moral concern than people who weren't told that.[25]

Following up on initial findings about the dementalization of animals used for food, researchers showed two groups of omnivores a picture of a cow and a sheep in a grassy field. One group was told that the animals were going to graze with other animals in a pasture and the other group that they were going to be slaughtered for food. When asked to evaluate the mental capacities of the animals, those who were told that they were to be eaten rated them as having lesser mental capabilities than those who were just told the animals would be grazing. This led the authors to conclude that meat eaters tend to deny mental capacity to the animals they eat.[26]

The denigration of animals also provides a model for the devaluation of women. As with ethnic prejudice, insulting characterizations of women as bitches, cows, sows, or old biddies show the connection between the two forms of prejudice.[27] Actually, the connection goes much deeper than that. Throughout history, men saw women as irrational beings driven by emotion and instinct, much like the stereotype used to subordinate animals. In the same way that animals have been considered inferior to humans, women have been seen as inferior to men and treated as property men could acquire. And, of course, they've also been exploited for their labor and reproductive capacity. As Catharine MacKinnon put it, "Women are the animals of the human kingdom, the mice of men's world."[28]

The Connection of Sexism and Speciesism

Research on the animalistic dehumanization of women provides evidence that sexism and speciesism are psychologically entangled and rooted in desires for group-based dominance and inequality. Furthermore, research on the symbolic value of meat corroborates its masculine value expressing dominance and power, and suggests that men who abstain from meat consumption (e.g., vegans) are feminized and devalued, particularly by those higher in sexism. We conclude that a greater recognition of the interconnected nature of patriarchal gender relations and practices of animal exploitation, including meat-eating, can help in efforts to improve the status of both women and animals.

Alina Salmen and Kristof Dhont, "Animalizing women and feminizing (vegan) men: The psychological intersections of sexism, speciesism, meat, and masculinity," *Social and Personality Psychology Compass* 17(2)(2023), e12717.

Once research began showing the connections between different forms of prejudice, social scientists began trying to determine why they're related. After a Social Dominance Scale was developed that reliably measures the extent to which people favor social dominance and inequality, researchers found that someone's Social Dominance Orientation strongly predicted whether they were generally prejudiced against members of different racial and ethnic minorities.[29] The reason for this, one social psychologist thought, was that people high in Social Dominance Orientation enjoy dominance, and less powerful minority groups provide easy targets to dominate.[30]

Animals, of course, also provide many opportunities for domination, and other studies have showed that people who were prejudiced against many ethnic groups were more likely to have negative attitudes about animals, too. As with generalized prejudice against different human groups, an underlying preference for social dominance and inequality underpinned prejudice against animals and helped explain why the different forms of bias are related.[31]

Subsequent research showed that people high in social dominance support dominating and exploiting the rest of the natural world, too.[32] They're more likely to endorse practices that unsustainably deplete natural resources and to deny the impact of human activities on climate change, an ideology called *ecological dominance*.[33] Research has converged from several directions, then, showing that social, human, and ecological dominance are related and that a preference for inequality connects all three.

The generalization of prejudice is commonly rooted in a belief that humans are fundamentally different from and superior to all other animals. For example, the English language version of an instrument used to measure someone's preference for ecological dominance includes a scale with two pictographs and these instructions:

Ideas on how humans, animals, and the natural environment should relate to each other can differ for every person. Using the image below as a guide, indicate which arrangement you personally think represents your own preference. There are no right or wrong answers here; we are simply interested in your personal preference. The more you move the slider to the right, the more you indicate a preference for a more hierarchical relationship between humans, animals, and the natural environment. The more you move the slider to the left, the more you indicate a preference for a less hierarchical relationship.[34]

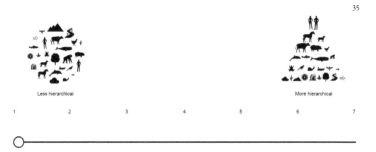

The two pictographs show the extent to which someone sees the world "through hierarchy-shaped glasses."[36] Believers in hierarchy and human supremacy favor the one on the right, which shows humans at the top of a pyramid with the rest of the natural world ranked in tiers below us. People who see the world with "egalitarian glasses" endorse the other image, which shows nature in an ecocentric circle with no hierarchy or rank.

* * *

As mentioned earlier, the devaluation of animals made it possible for supremacists to dehumanize disfavored groups of people and "treat them like animals."[37] Indeed, the very notion of *subhumanity*—that some people can be seen as *less than human*—depends on a belief in human supremacy.[38] In extreme cases, dehumanization has paved the way for genocides by providing their psychological lubricant. As one expert on dehumanization explained, "Time after time, genocide after genocide, they [perpetrators of atrocities] characterize those they wish to harm as less-than-human creatures, and in so doing diminish their moral status to such an extent as to make the commission of the most hideous acts of violence against them permissible or even obligatory."[39] Suggestions that some people should be treated as subhuman—that Jewish people should be exterminated like rats or Rwandan Tutsis wiped out like cockroaches—were based on the reduced moral protections we afford other animals.

Believing that we're superior to other animals depends on also believing that we're fundamentally different from them, because ranking groups by value requires seeing them as categorically different from each other.[40] Our need to see ourselves as different from and superior to all other animals is so strong that we've redefined the word *animal* to exclude us and given the word a negative connotation.

History has shown that supremacists pass their most convincing myths about disfavored groups down from one generation to the next. Attempts to unmask them elicit a strong pushback, as discussed in the chapter about the disparagement of critics. If the prevailing myths are successfully challenged, though, dominant groups often put together more socially acceptable ones that maintain the hierarchy with greater subtlety.

This happened with myths about stigmatized racial and ethnic groups. At one time, prejudice against them was so widely accepted that opinions about their inferiority were straightforward. As late as 1906, the president of the United States, Theodore Roosevelt, wrote to a friend that "as to the Negroes, . . . I entirely agree with you that as a race and in the mass they are altogether inferior to the whites."[41] Modern supremacists usually avoid such overt claims of inferiority. They may say that subordinate groups are different from a dominant one and the difference explains their lack of achievement. American white supremacists can say that African Americans are more likely to live in poverty than whites because they lack a strong Protestant work ethic,[42] and Canadians may say that "[i]f Native Indians are less well-off, it's because they don't work hard enough."[43]

Sexist myths and stereotypes have gone through a similar evolution. A nineteenth-century French psychologist repeated a hostile version, reporting in a professional journal that "[a]ll psychologists who have studied the intelligence of women . . . recognize today that they represent the most inferior forms of human evolution and that they are closer to children and savages than to an adult, civilized man."[44] By now, most male supremacists endorse a more benevolent view of women, portraying them as having a purity and warmth that needs protection.[45] While this version seems positive, it suggests that women are more suited to roles as homemakers and childcare workers than as leaders in business or government, hiding male domination behind "a façade of pleasantry."[46]

Human supremacists have developed more subtle, benevolent myths, too. As discussed earlier, one of the most common is the Myth of Happy Meat,[47] in which all the animals on a "humane" farm lead a happy life and have a merciful death.[48] Methods of disengagement make it easier for myths like this to gain traction. As discussed earlier, the meat industry hides the harm it inflicts by locating production facilities and slaughterhouses in remote locations, and most consumers are content to hide *from* the harm.

The Myth of Happy Meat has many variations. Egg producers who don't keep hens in battery cages often promote their eggs as *cage-free*, suggesting that they humanely raise the hens. Whether they keep hens in a cage, however, is only one part of the care that egg producers provide to the animals they raise. They may treat the animals well in one way and poorly in another, cramming cage-free hens into a dark warehouse instead of a cage. Producers can also amputate part of a cage-free hen's toes, which can cause chronic, long-term pain.[49]

Other egg producers market their products as *free-range*. While hens from these producers may have access to the outdoors, the range can be barren. The birds may also be from breeds selected for high egg production, making it more likely they'll suffer from osteoporosis due to calcium depletion and be unable to use any range at all.

Some farmers who raise chickens for meat also say the chickens are *free-range*. Birds from a fast-growing breed, though, may not be able to make much use of a range because they've grown so fast that they're lame. Slower-growing birds may be able to make better use of a range but will likely end their lives the same way as the faster-growing ones, being killed at an early age. Even though they're usually allowed to live longer than the faster-growing birds, slow-growing ones are usually killed when only about twelve weeks old.

It's much the same for turkeys marketed as *free-range*. Those from varieties bred for fast growth are even more likely than fast-growing chickens to have painful leg problems that greatly limit their ability to use any range. Free-range turkeys may also have had part of their toes amputated, which causes pain for at least several days.[50] Even if producers raise varieties of turkeys not prone to the compromised welfare of broad-breasted ones, the economics of production still lead them to cut the birds' lives short, usually having them slaughtered when only about seven months old, a fraction of their natural life span.[51]

Some pork producers say that pigs on their farms are *humanely raised*. Although the producers may not confine the sows in metal crates for most of their lives, they may keep them in a closely packed shed without access to the outdoors. Even pigs raised in pastures may have had their tail amputated, and the males may have been castrated without anesthesia. Pasture-raised pigs not kept for breeding are usually slaughtered when only about six months old, long before they're even fully grown.

Beef producers commonly say that their cattle are *grass-fed*, suggesting that they grazed in bucolic pastures throughout their lives. Often this isn't the case. In the United States, as long as cattle have grazed in pastures for at least half of their life, they can legally be called grass-fed. Often grass-fed cattle begin their life grazing in a pasture and finish it in an industrial feedlot. Even cattle that live in pastures throughout their life can be branded, dehorned, and castrated without anesthesia. And they're usually slaughtered in the same terrifying way as cattle finished in a feedlot.[52]

Although many claims that people make regarding the humane treatment of animals are vague or meaningless, not all of them are. Several animal welfare groups encourage producers to avoid the cruelest farming methods by offering seals of approval like Certified Humane or American Humane Certified. While these standards of care prohibit practices like stuffing hens in battery cages or keeping sows in crates so small they can't even turn around, they allow other inhumane practices, like confining chickens, pigs, and turkeys in sheds throughout their life, finishing cattle in feedlots, and taking calves from cows used in the dairy industry shortly after the calves are born.

In the end, almost all meat producers have animals slaughtered when they're very young because that's when their flesh is worth the most. If the animals on "humane" farms are living a life filled with happiness—as the Myth of Happy Meat goes—that doesn't justify taking the best part of their happy life from them. Just the opposite. It's a good reason *not* to kill them and thus deprive them of the future happiness they might have enjoyed.[53]

Defenders of animal experimentation have developed a similar benevolent myth: the Myth of Humane Animal Research. In 2007, a spokesperson for the Coalition for Animal Research Education advised scientists who conduct research on animals to describe animal research as *humane* "whenever possible."[54] Often that's not possible. Humane people show "kindness, care, and sympathy toward others, especially those who are suffering."[55] Researchers often show little compassion for animals who are suffering. Instead, they make them suffer by drowning, suffocating, starving, or blinding them, damaging their brains, severing their limbs, crushing their organs, and inducing heart attacks, paralysis, and seizures.[56] They also cause them to suffer from heart disease, many types of cancer, Parkinson's disease, Huntington's disease, amyotrophic lateral sclerosis (ALS), and Alzheimer's disease.

In 1959, two scholars working for a British animal welfare organization published *The Principles of Humane Experimental Technique*, setting forth animal research standards that became known as the 3 Rs: *replacing* sentient animals with other models when possible, *reducing* the number used to the minimum required for statistical adequacy, and *refining* techniques to reduce the animals' suffering.[57] In the same way that standards like Certified Humane try to get meat, dairy, and egg producers not to use the most inhumane practices, the 3 Rs were intended to increase the humanity of animal research.[58] In many ways, they did.

One contribution that the authors of *The Principles* made was to add hunger and bodily discomfort to the list of harms that animals can suffer when used in laboratories.[59] While their list of harms was more complete than earlier ones, it was still quite incomplete. It failed to consider confinement as a harm even though animals are confined when kept in a laboratory and confinement causes them to suffer distress.[60] Another shortcoming of the book was its failure to include any upper limits on the harm that can humanely be inflicted on the animals. Without any limits, projects can be considered humane even if they cause animals to suffer harms so great that their lives are no longer worth living.

Almost all animal research harms the animals used.[61] If the harm makes their life no longer worth living, that exceeds the limit of suffering that can reasonably be considered *humane*. If the harm hasn't reached that point and the animal's life continues to be worth living, then killing the animal isn't humane because it deprives the animal of future pleasurable experiences. Either way—whether the animal's life continues to be worth living or not—animal research that includes killing the subjects (as almost all of it does) can't be considered *humane* without depriving the word of any meaning, another example of the exonerative corruption of language discussed in the first chapter.

We know it's wrong for dominant individuals to harm others. We also know it's wrong for members of a stronger group to exploit those from other groups, no matter how great the benefit their own group may enjoy. At some level, we must know that meat isn't happy and animal research isn't humane; otherwise, we wouldn't be driven to come up with all the excuses, rationalizations, and justifications for them that have been discussed throughout this book.

❦ 10 ❧

Overcoming Interconnected Prejudices

> "Aristotle thought that men were naturally superior to women and Greeks naturally superior to other races; Victorians thought white men had to shoulder the burden of being superior to savages; and Nazis thought Aryans were a master race. We have now come to reject these and many other supposedly natural hierarchies; the history of what we consider moral progress can be viewed as, in large part, the replacement of hierarchical worldviews with a presumption in favor of forms of egalitarianism."
>
> —**S. F. Sapontzis**, *Morals, Reason, and Animals* (Philadelphia: Temple University Press, 1987), 107.

The interconnections between different forms of prejudice suggest that they have common roots.[1] Why else would prejudiced attitudes generalize from one devalued group to another when the groups are often quite different? Why is someone who is anti-Jewish more likely to be anti-Catholic, too, and anti-Negro, anti-women, anti-animal, and anti-environment? Studies regarding the common roots of different prejudices have begun to provide some answers to these questions.

These studies have consistently shown that beliefs in social inequality and group-based dominance are key factors in the generalization of prejudice.[2,3] This shouldn't be surprising. Different forms of prejudice share the same three beliefs: that members of one group are qualitatively different from members of all other groups, superior to them, and entitled to dominate them.

Research has also shown that support for an authoritarian form of conservative governance contributes to the generalization of prejudice.[4] This shouldn't be surprising either. Conservatives generally prefer maintaining traditional social arrangements and, as the quotation at the beginning of the chapter mentions, social domination by one supremacist group or another has been common throughout human history, as have authoritarian rulers driven to preserve their power and privileges.

Beliefs in social dominance and authoritarian governance contribute more than any other factors to the generalization of prejudice,[5] but other factors contribute, too. Prejudiced attitudes are strongly related to lower levels of empathy.[6] This makes sense, too. Concern for others' well-being can make someone more likely to empathize with the victims of discrimination and appreciate their concerns.[7]

Gender plays a role, too. Women tend to be less prejudiced than men, largely because they're likely to be more empathic.[8] They also tend to be less dominance-oriented and are often victims of discrimination themselves, which may lead them to be less prejudiced.[9]

Recent research has shed more light on the roots of generalized prejudice. In a set of eight studies, researchers tried to determine whether a belief in evolution is connected in some way to prejudice and discriminatory behavior. They analyzed survey data from a diverse group of countries—the United States, Israel, nineteen Eastern European countries, and twenty-five predominantly Muslim countries—and found that people who believe that humans evolved from animals tended to be less prejudiced than those who don't believe in evolution; this was true even after the researchers separated out contributions made by a respondent's religiosity, political ideology, and educational level.[10] It may be, the authors suggested, that believers in evolution recognize that all humans share the same evolutionary background, leading them to have more empathy for people from other groups and more positive attitudes toward them.[11]

In some of the countries studied, more than a third of the survey respondents said they didn't believe in human evolution.[12] Why would anyone believe that humans haven't evolved from other animals when the evidence is so clear that we have? For that matter, why would anyone believe that one ethnic or racial group is categorically different from and superior to all other groups or that men are superior to women when these beliefs aren't based in fact either? As discussed next, part of the answer may lie in the thirst for exploitation, which drives all supremacist ideologies.

The false beliefs that form the core of supremacist ideologies begin with the creation of an artificial divide to separate one group from all the others.[13] Supremacists need to believe their group is different from all the others so they can give it elite status.[14] Otherwise, giving themselves special privileges would run afoul of the moral principle mentioned in the last chapter that it's unfair to treat individuals differently unless there's a difference that justifies the unequal treatment.[15]

Finding a quality that makes one group qualitatively different from similar ones can be challenging. The search for a line that divides humans from all other animals is a good example. Evolutionary processes make it difficult to separate humans from all other animals, because we've evolved together with them and, as discussed in the previous chapter, all capacities previously thought to make us unique have been found in some other species, too.

For supremacists, it isn't enough to believe that their group is different from all others; they need to believe it's superior. They use circular reasoning to get there, pointing to a quality they say makes their group unique and then using it to determine a group's moral status. The belief in human supremacy again provides a good example. Human supremacists frequently base their claim of superiority on human intelligence, equating intelligence with cognitive complexity even though that's only one aspect of intelligence. Less chauvinistically, intelligence can be seen as a set of abilities that enable individuals to adapt well to their particular environment.[16] Living in different environments, each species adapts differently. As Frans de Waal suggested, it wouldn't be fair to measure squirrels' intelligence by considering how well they can count to ten when counting is not what their life is all about. Instead, we should consider how well they can retrieve buried nuts and think of that as a different form of intelligence.[17]

Now we come to the final supremacist fallacy, the belief that their group's superiority entitles it to dominate all those from other groups.[18] Although it's the third one, a penchant for exploitation drives the first two. Beliefs that their group is different from and superior to all other groups are just moral justifications for the supremacists' exploitation of the other groups. And their craving for exploitation pulls so strongly that supremacists are driven to adopt beliefs that are plainly false.

* * *

The interconnections between different forms of prejudice make it more difficult to overcome any one of them individually because, as discussed throughout this book, they support and reinforce each other.[19] As one pair of researchers commented, "Efforts to tackle one form of prejudice or bias become a game of whack-a-mole if we do not address how such systems of oppression are systematically linked."[20] Interventions that effectively target the roots of supremacist ideologies, though, can reach well beyond any single form of prejudice.[21] With that in mind, here are some things we can do to fight all forms of prejudice by addressing their common roots.

1. **Support groups and programs that fight many forms of oppression.** Just as different forms of prejudice have common roots, different forms of discriminatory behavior do, too.[22] Dominant groups frequently oppress many other groups, often in the same way. As mentioned earlier, male supremacists devalue women by comparing them to animals—another group they denigrate—and white supremacists do the same to Blacks. When oppressed groups fail to work together against a common oppressor, that makes it easier for a dominant group to continue oppressing each of them and harder for each one to eradicate the form that most directly affects its members. All too often, though, advocacy groups fight one form of oppression while practicing another. Organizations that work to protect animals,[23] the environment,[24] or oppressed racial groups[25] commonly employ patriarchal practices and devalue the work of women.[26] And White people usually dominate groups that advocate for women,[27] animals,[28] or the rest of the natural world.[29] Because different forms of prejudice reinforce each other, groups fighting for social equality can't succeed if they don't practice it themselves.

   The narrow focus of advocacy groups is beginning to change. More and more of them, including Greenpeace and the United Nations Environmental Programme, are taking a broad approach to fighting oppression by embracing gender and racial diversity in their leadership and operations. These groups deserve our support. We can make contributions to them and work to have our country increase the funding it provides to the U.N. Environment Programme.[30]

2. **Help achieve gender equality.** It's been a man's world. For thousands of years, men have dominated women and excluded them from positions of power.[31] It's also been a violent world, torn for millennia by strife between different racial, ethnic, religious, and national groups. The two are related.

Throughout the world, men are more aggressive than women.[32] They're also much more likely to perpetrate the worst forms of aggression, including homicide and war.[33] As mentioned earlier, men tend to be more prejudiced than women, too. Adding to this toxic mix, they tend to be more supportive of social inequality and group-based dominance,[34] ideologies that foster tribalism and conflict between groups. In addition, early in life boys become more comfortable with using methods of moral disengagement to avoid feeling guilty for antisocial behavior than girls do,[35] a tendency that continues into adulthood.[36] If we can achieve equality between the genders, then our world won't only be more equitable, it will be more peaceful as well.

More than forty years ago, the United Nations adopted the Convention on the Elimination of All Forms of Discrimination Against Women, requiring its members to do whatever is needed to make sure that women have rights equal to those that men enjoy. By now, almost every country has committed itself to doing that.[37] Despite their commitments, however, most countries still have discriminatory laws that prevent women and girls from enjoying basic human rights.[38] These laws entrench inequality and signify that gender-based discrimination is socially acceptable.[39]

Women have an equal right to participate in government,[40] and in recent years more and more of them have begun participating in political affairs. At the current rate, though, it will take another forty years for women to achieve parity with men in national legislatures.[41] We can speed this up by voting for candidates who pledge to support the repeal of gender-discriminatory laws. We can also support the foremost global champion of gender equality, U.N. Women, and work to have our country increase the support it provides to that organization.[42]

3. **Support multicultural education programs for children.** People throughout the world tend to believe that their culture is more important and valuable than any other culture.[43] This commonly leads them to be prejudiced against people from other cultures and hostile to them.[44] Children commonly adopt these prejudiced attitudes by the time they're five years old.[45]

In his treatise on prejudice, Gordon Allport predicted that under the right conditions contact between people from different groups can reduce prejudice and conflict between the groups.[46] Since that time, hundreds of studies undertaken all over the world have confirmed Allport's theory.[47] While most of these studies involved adolescents and adults, more than eighty involved children.[48] Many of these studies found that even indirect or virtual contact with people from other groups can lead children to have more positive attitudes toward them. For example, studies that included more than 10,000 children from fifteen countries found that watching productions of the children's television show *Sesame Street*—which highlighted friendships and other positive relationships between people from different backgrounds—was associated with the children's having more positive attitudes toward people from stigmatized groups, even in areas troubled by long-standing group-based hostility.[49]

To foster positive changes in children's attitudes toward people from other groups, though, multicultural education programs must go beyond just describing diversity or having multicultural festivals.[50] They need to embrace cultural diversity and the contributions people from different cultures can make to counter the belief that one particular culture is superior to all others.

We can support multicultural education by being advocates for these programs in our community, having our children participate in them, and when possible, having children watch programs and read stories about positive interactions between people from different backgrounds.

4. **Follow a plant-based diet**. In our everyday lives, most of us don't have a chance to repudiate supremacism and the toxic idea that it's alright for a strong group to dominate and exploit others. The simple act of deciding what to eat, though, gives us a chance to do that every day. If you oppose any of the interconnected forms of prejudice—whether in the form of white supremacism, male supremacism, or human supremacism—you can be true to your best values and avoid consuming products taken from animals.

The same applies if you think of yourself as a humane person. Or an environmentalist. Or a feminist. Or a humanitarian. Farmers routinely mutilate the animals they use, confine them throughout their lives, and have them slaughtered in their youth, yet people with humane values still buy their products. Environmentalists do, too, despite the environmental devastation caused by animal agriculture. Feminists buy eggs and dairy products even though producers relentlessly exploit the reproductive capacity of female animals and destroy their families. Humanitarians continue to eat meat, although meat production diverts enormous amounts of grain and soy that hungry people could use to nourish themselves and drives up the cost of that which remains (for extended discussions about an omnivore's various moral conflicts, please see "The Omnivore's Moral Dilemmas" in the Appendix).

If you despise the many forms of supremacism or think of yourself as a humane person, a feminist, an environmentalist, or a humanitarian, you can walk the talk by following a plant-based diet.

Appendix

THE OMNIVORE'S MORAL DILEMMAS

In his 2006 book, *The Omnivore's Dilemma,* Michael Pollan told how he became a vegetarian because he didn't want to be complicit in the great suffering that factory farm operators inflict on the animals they raise. In the shadow of factory farms, he wrote, it didn't seem far-fetched to think that history will judge those who eat meat from these farms as harshly as it judges the Germans who went about their lives in the shadow of Treblinka.[1]

He returned to eating meat, though, after seeing animals on a small farm enjoying their lives, the hens foraging in a pasture and the pigs rooting around in a barn looking for kernels of corn in a cake of compost. As he put it: "In the same way we can probably recognize animal suffering when we see it, animal happiness is unmistakable, too, and during my week on the farm I saw it in abundance."[2] In the end, he decided it was all right to eat meat from a farm like the one he visited.

The happiness Pollan saw on that farm, though, is the reason why it's wrong to consume products from a "happy farm," too. Most people think that if the staff at an animal shelter put a young, healthy dog or cat to death—even if their death is pain-free—it raises moral concerns. Animals raised for food on farms are sentient, too,[3] and taking the lives of young, healthy farmed animals raises similar concerns. Pollan was right when he said it mattered when we cause a sentient animal to suffer. He was wrong, though, when he said it didn't matter when we take a healthy sentient animal's life.[4]

Although Pollan devoted a chapter in his book to the ethics of eating animals, he failed to consider many of the significant issues it raises. The following articles will consider some of them, addressing questions like:

- Can someone eat meat and still be a genuine environmentalist or a true feminist or humanitarian?
- Do animals raised on fish farms suffer any less than animals raised on other industrial farms?
- Are eggs and dairy products free of the bloodshed that taints meat production?

THE ENVIRONMENTALIST OMNIVORE'S MORAL DILEMMA

According to a 2006 report from the United Nations Food and Agriculture Organization, animal agriculture casts a "long shadow."[5] As discussed later, it pollutes the planet's air and water, degrades its land, reduces its biodiversity, and contributes significantly to climate change. All told, animal agriculture is one of the top two or three contributors to the most serious environmental problems at every scale, from local to global.[6]

Animal agriculture produces enormous amounts of waste that can leach from farmland and escape from lagoons and holding ponds. In their 2006 report, environmental scientists from the Food and Agriculture Organization concluded that livestock production probably causes more water pollution than any other type of human activity.[7]

Waste from livestock operations can volatilize and pollute the air, too. Animal agriculture also contributes significantly to acid rain and the acidification of ecosystems by producing almost two-thirds of the ammonia generated by human activity.[8]

In addition to the pollution it causes, animal agriculture uses enormous quantities of water, an increasingly scarce resource. Producing a kilogram of animal protein uses about 100 times more water than producing a kilogram of protein from grain.[9] Livestock also reduce the replenishment of freshwater by compacting soil, reducing infiltration, degrading the banks of watercourses, drying up floodplains, and lowering water tables.[10]

Besides polluting and depleting our planet's finite natural resources, animal agriculture severely damages its ecosystems. It may cause more loss of biodiversity than any other human activity.[11]

Of all the environmental harms caused by animal agriculture, its disproportionate contribution to climate change will likely be the most severe over the long term. Global warming is the most serious environmental challenge facing humanity,[12] and the production of meat, eggs, and dairy products emits far more greenhouse gases per serving than vegetables or grain.

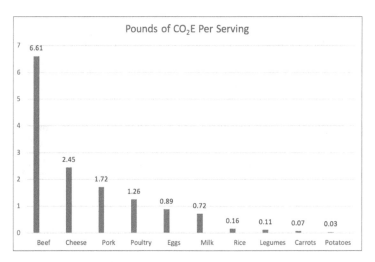

Figure 2: "Carbon Footprint Factsheet," Center for Sustainable Systems, accessed on January 28, 2024. https://css.umich.edu/publications/factsheets/sustainability-indicators/carbon-footprint-factsheet

Even grass-fed beef[13] and farmed animals raised according to organic standards[14] have a much larger carbon footprint than vegetables or grain. In 2016, the world's twenty largest meat and dairy producers generated 932 metric tons of greenhouse gas emissions; if they were a country, these producers would be the world's seventh largest greenhouse gas emitter.[15]

Because animal agriculture causes such great environmental harm, following a plant-based diet is one of the most effective things we can do to protect our planet and all who live here. According to the Barilla Center for Food and Nutrition, omnivores who adopt a vegetarian diet reduce their dietary contribution to global warming by almost two-thirds.[16]

It turns out that someone can be an omnivore or a genuine environmentalist. They can't be both.

Best Diet to Protect the Environment

"A vegan diet is probably the single biggest way to reduce your impact on planet Earth, not just greenhouse gases, but global acidification, eutrophication, land use, and water use."

—**Joseph Poore**, lead author of an Oxford University study of 38,700 farms in 119 countries: "Reducing food's environmental impacts through producers and consumers," *Science* 360 (6392), 987–992. *The Guardian,* May 31, 2018.

THE FEMINIST OMNIVORE'S MORAL DILEMMA

Women have been dominated and exploited throughout history. Female farmed animals have been, too. And still are.

Factory-farmed turkeys, for instance, have been bred to have such an oversized breast that they can't mate naturally, so producers have them artificially inseminated. Here's a description of how that's done:

> In the hen house, our job was to "break" the hens. You grab a hen by the legs, trying to cross both "ankles" in order to hold her feet and legs with one hand. The hens weigh 20 to 30 pounds and are terrified, beating their wings and struggling in panic. . . . Once you have grabbed her with one hand, you flop her down chest first on the edge of a pit with the tail end sticking up. You put your free hand over the vent and tail and pull the rump and tail feathers upward. At the same time, you pull the hand holding the feet downward, thus "breaking" the hen so that her rear is straight up and her vent open.[17]

Then another worker inseminates the hen pneumatically with semen from a straw.

On intensive hog farms, sows are usually restrained and artificially inseminated, too. And cows on intensive dairy farms are often artificially inseminated while restrained in a steel frame some critics call a "rape rack."

On most dairy farms, calves are taken from their mothers shortly after they're born. Producers do this to make more money because the milk that calves would nurse from their mothers is worth more than the milk replacer and dry feed they provide to the calf. Males not kept for breeding end up being slaughtered for beef or veal.

Industrial producers also take newborns from sows and hens used to produce meat. And large-scale egg producers take male chicks from their mothers and kill those not kept for breeding.

Animal agriculture is tainted by these flagrant violations of female animals. No one has to eat meat, eggs, or dairy products. Like the rest of us, feminists get to decide if they want to participate in a system stained by the domination and exploitation of females.

> "If we heard of an alien civilization that takes babies away from mothers, eats the babies, and also consumes the mother's milk, we would probably not want to meet them."
>
> —**Jonathan Balcombe**, *Second Nature: The Inner Lives of Animals* (New York: Palgrave Macmillan, 2010), 203.

THE HUMANITARIAN OMNIVORE'S MORAL DILEMMA

Proponents of intensive animal agriculture commonly claim that its efficiencies allow industrial operators to produce food so inexpensively that people with limited incomes can afford to buy meat.[18] Actually, it's just the opposite—meat production often makes it more likely that poor people will go hungry. To generate much-needed revenue, many countries export grain to wealthier countries that they could use to feed hungry people in their own country. India is an excellent example. Although it ranked 94th among 107 countries in the Global Hunger Index, in 2019 it exported animal feed worth $232 million to other countries[19] while 14 percent of its population was undernourished and chronic malnutrition had stunted the growth of 37.4 percent of its children under the age of five.[20]

Every time someone buys meat, they participate in a system where people living in richer countries take what they want from people living in poorer ones, whether those living there need it or not. Humanitarians can decide whether they want to participate in this agricultural colonialism.

> "The cattle of the rich steal the bread of the poor." —**Mohandas Gandhi**
>
> —**Jeremy MacClancy**, *Consuming Culture: Why You Eat What You Eat* (New York: Henry Holt, 1992), 150.

THE HUMANE PESCATARIAN'S MORAL DILEMMA

It may seem like it's more ethical to eat fish than animals raised on terrestrial farms because at least fish live free until they're caught. By now, though, more than half of the fish people eat never swim free;[21] they're raised on aquatic farms and confined all their life.

In many ways, fish farms are like factory farms. Industry standards are guided by economics. The stress and suffering the fish endure are only considered if they affect profitability. As with factory farms, the animals are confined so densely they can't escape from other animals who bully or cannibalize them.

In some ways, fish raised on aquatic farms have it worse than animals on land-based ones, where the animals are usually protected from predators. On a fish farm, though, the fish fall prey to birds, seals, and other carnivores. Some operators even stock their farms with predator fish to reduce population densities that can lead to stunted growth. Disease, parasites, predation, and aggression produce death rates of ten to thirty percent on fish farms, rates that wouldn't be accepted on a land-based farm.[22]

When they're slaughtered, farmed fish are frequently killed in brutal ways that would be illegal if used on cows or pigs. Sometimes, they're just taken out of the water and left to suffocate. One biologist compared this to killing chickens by throwing them in a tank of water and waiting for them to drown.[23]

In addition, the suffering of wild-caught fish taints farmed fish, too, because they're fed fishmeal and fish oil from wild-caught ones. The form of suffering inflicted on wild fish depends on the way they're caught and slaughtered. In longline fishing, live fish are impaled on hooks attached to lines set in the water. When other fish take the bait, they become impaled themselves and languish there for hours, even days, until the lines are hauled in. All the while, they may be attacked by sharks and other predators.[24]

When trawlers are used, fish are squeezed together at the tail end of a bag-shaped net dragged behind the boat. Many suffocate in the crush. Others suffer a similar fate when a school is encircled by a seine net hauled behind a boat, and they're crushed at the end of the net when it's drawn together and hauled to the surface.[25]

While the form of suffering varies depending on how fish are caught in the wild or raised on a farm, one thing remains constant. As Jonathan Safran Foer put it, "You never have to wonder if the fish on your plate had to suffer. It did."[26]

THE HUMANE VEGETARIAN'S MORAL DILEMMA

People may think it's more ethical to consume eggs and dairy products than meat because at least they can be produced without bloodshed. Michael Pollan believed that at first, writing in *The Omnivore's Dilemma* that "... eggs and milk can be coaxed from animals without hurting or killing them—or so at least I thought."[27] In the book, Pollan told how, when he looked more closely, he found that hens used for egg production in America were "piled together with a half-dozen other hens in a wire cage the floor of which four pages of this book could carpet wall to wall. Every natural instinct of this hen is thwarted, leading to a range of behavioral 'vices' that can include cannibalizing her cage mates and rubbing her breast against the wire mesh until it is completely bald and bleeding." He went on to write ". . . what you see when you look is the cruelty—and the blindness to cruelty—required to produce eggs that can be sold for seventy-nine cents a dozen."[28]

There's bloodshed in egg production, too. Every year, millions of male chicks born to laying hens are killed shortly after they emerge from their shells because they're of little value to a producer.

In time, the bloodshed reaches the hens themselves. After laying an egg a day for a year or two, many hens are emaciated and poorly feathered.[29] Then farmers often just kill them and dispose of their bodies, referring to them, with brutal realism, as "spent."[30]

There's blood in the milk from dairy operations, too. Males born to dairy cows are sold for meat unless kept for breeding.

When you look closely, it turns out that the production of eggs and dairy products is just as inhumane as meat production, sometimes even more so. People can decide whether they want to participate in this inhumanity by consuming eggs or dairy products.

Bibliography

Adams, Carol J., and Josephine Donovan, eds. *Animals and Women: Feminist Theoretical Explorations*. Durham, North Carolina: Duke University Press, 1995.

——. *The Sexual Politics of Meat: A Feminist-Vegetarian Critical Theory*. New York: Continuum, 1996.

Akhtar, Sahar. "Animal Pain and Welfare: Can Pain Sometimes Be Worse for Them than for Us?" in *The Oxford Handbook of Animal Ethics*, Tom L. Beauchamp and R. G. Frey, eds. Oxford: Oxford University Press, 2011.

Akrami, Nazar, Bo Ekehammar, and Robin Bergh. "Generalized Prejudice: Common and Specific Components." *Psychological Science* 22, no. 1 (2011).

Albersmeier, Frauke. "Speciesism and Speciescentrism." *Ethical Theory and Moral Practice* 24 (2021), 511-527.

Allport, Gordon. *The Nature of Prejudice*. Reading, Massachusetts: Addison-Wesley, 1979.

Altemeyer, Bob. "The Other 'Authoritarian Personality,'" in *Political Psychology*, John J. Jost and Jim Sidanius, eds. New York: Psychology Press, 2004.

Arluke, Arnold. "Sacrificial Symbolism in Animal Experimentation: Object or Pet?" *Anthrozoös* 2, no. 2 (1988).

——. "Getting into the Closet with Science: Information Control Among Animal Experimenters." *Journal of Contemporary Ethnography* 20, no. 3 (1991).

———. "Trapped in a Guilt Cage," *New Scientist* 134, no. 1815 (1992).

Armstrong, Susan, and Richard Botzler, eds. *The Animal Ethics Reader*, 3rd ed. New York: Routledge, 2017.

AVMA Guidelines for the Euthanasia of Animals: 2020 Edition. Schaumburg, Illinois: American Veterinary Medical Association, 2020.

Backström, Martin, and Fredrik Björklund. "Structural Modeling of Generalized Prejudice: The Role of Social Dominance, Authoritarianism, and Empathy." *Journal of Individual Differences* 28, no. 1 (2007).

Baker, Ron. *The American Hunting Myth*. New York: Vantage Press, 1985.

Balcombe, Jonathan. *Second Nature: The Inner Lives of Animals*. New York: Palgrave Macmillan, 2010.

———. *What a Fish Knows: The Inner Lives of Our Underwater Cousins*. New York: Farrar, Straus, and Giroux, 2016.

Bandura, Albert. "Moral Disengagement in the Perpetration of Inhumanities." *Personality and Social Psychology Review* 3, no. 3 (1999).

———. "Selective Moral Disengagement in the Exercise of Moral Agency." *Journal of Moral Education* 31, no. 2 (2002).

———. "Impeding Ecological Sustainability Through Selective Moral Disengagement." *International Journal of Innovation and Sustainable Development* 2, no. 1 (2009).

———. *Moral Disengagement: How People Do Harm and Live With Themselves*. New York: Worth Publishers, 2016.

Bandura, Albert, Bill Underwood, and Michael E. Fromson. "Disinhibition of Aggression through Diffusion of Responsibility and Dehumanization of Victims." *Journal of Research in Personality* 9, no. 4 (1975).

James A. Banks, ed. *The Routledge International Companion to Multicultural Education*. New York: Routledge, 2009.

Bartal, Inbal Ben-Ami, Jean Decety, and Peggy Mason. "Empathy and Pro-Social Behavior in Rats." *Science* 334, no. 6061 (2011).

Bass, Robert. "Lives in the Balance: Utilitarianism and Animal Research," in *The Ethics of Animal Research: Exploring the Controversy*, Jeremy R. Garrett, ed. Cambridge, Massachusetts: MIT Press, 2012.

Bastian, Brock, Kimberly Costello, Steve Loughnan, and Gordon Hodson. "When Closing the Human-Animal Divide Expands Moral Concern: The Importance of Framing." *Social Psychological and Personality Science* 3, no. 4 (2012).

Bastian, Brock, and Steve Loughnan. "Resolving the Meat-Paradox: A Motivational Account of Morally Troubling Behavior and Its Maintenance." *Personality and Social Psychology Review* 21, no. 3 (2016).

Bastian, Brock, Steve Loughnan, Nick Haslam, and Helena R. M. Radke. "Don't Mind Meat? The Denial of Mind to Animals Used for Human Consumption." *Personality and Social Psychology Bulletin* 38, no. 2 (2012).

Baysinger, Angela, Michael Senn, Jordan Gebhardt, Christopher Rademacher, and Monique Pairis-Garcia. "A Case Study of Ventilation Shutdown with the Addition of High Temperature and Humidity for Depopulation of Pigs." *Journal of the American Veterinary Medical Association* 259, no. 4 (2021).

Baxter, Seaton. *Intensive Pig Production: Environmental Management and Design*. London: Granada, 1984.

Beauchamp, Tom, and David DeGrazia. *Principles of Animal Research Ethics*. New York: Oxford University Press, 2020.

Beauchamp, Tom, and R. G. Frey, eds. *The Oxford Handbook of Animal Ethics*. Oxford: Oxford University Press, 2011.

Beer, Christopher Todd. " Climate Justice: the Global South and Policy Preferences of Kenyan Environmental NGOs." *The Global South* 8, no. 2 (2014).

Bekoff, Marc, and Carron Meaney, eds. *Encyclopedia of Animal Rights and Animal Welfare*. Chicago: Fitzroy Dearborn, 1998.

Bekoff, Marc, and Jessica Pierce. *Wild Justice: The Moral Lives of Animals*. Chicago: University of Chicago Press, 2009.

Bell, Karen. "Bread and Roses: A Gender Perspective on Environmental Justice and Public Health." *International Journal of Environmental Research and Public Health* 13, no. 10 (2016).

Berg, Robert, and David Halvorson. *Turkey Management Guide*. St. Paul, Minnesota: Turkey Growers Association, 1985.

Bermond, Bob. "A Neuropsychological and Evolutionary Approach to Animal Consciousness and Animal Suffering," in *The Animal Ethics Reader*, 3rd ed., Susan Armstrong and Richard Botzler, eds. New York: Routledge, 2017.

Bizumic, Boris, and John Duckitt. "What Is and Is Not Ethnocentrism? A Conceptual Analysis and Political Implications." *Political Psychology* 33, no. 6 (2012).

Borkfelt, Sune, Sara Kondrup, Helena Röcklinsberg, Kristian Bjørkdahl and Mickey Gjerris. "Closer to Nature? A Critical Discussion of the Marketing of 'Ethical' Animal Products." *Journal of Agricultural and Environmental Ethics* 28, no. 6 (2015).

Bourdain, Anthony. *Kitchen Confidential: Adventures in the Culinary Underbelly.* New York: Bloomsbury, 2000.

Braithwaite, Victoria. *Do Fish Feel Pain?* Oxford: Oxford University Press, 2010.

Bratanova, Boyka, Steve Loughnan, and Brock Bastian. "The Effect of Categorization as Food on the Perceived Moral Standing of Animals." *Appetite* 57, no. 1 (2011).

Brown, Sue Ellen. "The Under-representation of African American Employees in Animal Welfare Organizations in the United States." *Society and Animals* 13, no. 2 (2005).

Browning, Christopher. *Ordinary Men: Reserve Battalion 101 and the Final Solution in Poland.* New York: Harper Collins, 2017.

Buettinger, Craig. "Antivivisection and the Charge of Zoophil-psychosis in the Early Twentieth Century." *The Historian* 55, no. 2 (1995).

Byrnes, J. "Raising Pigs by the Calendar at Maplewood Farm." *Hog Farm Management,* (September 1976).

Carter, Alan. "Animals, Pain and Morality." *Journal of Applied Philosophy* 22, no. 1 (2005).

Cartwright, S.A. "On the Caucasians and the Africans," in *Cotton Is King and Pro-Slavery Arguments*. Oxford: Benediction Classics, 2011.

Caviola, Lucius, Jim A. C. Everett, and Nadira S. Faber. "The Moral Standing of Animals: Towards a Psychology of Speciesism." *Journal of Personality and Social Psychology* 116, no. 6 (2019).

Caviola, Lucius, Stefan Schubert, Guy Kahane, and Nadira S. Faber. "Humans First: Why People Value Animals Less than Humans." *Cognition* 225 (2022).

Cesarani, David. *Becoming Eichmann: Rethinking the Life, Crimes, and Trial of a 'Desk Murderer.'* New York: Da Capo Press, 2004.

Chen, Jun. "Empathy for Distress in Humans and Rodents." *Neuroscience Bulletin* 34, no. 1 (2018).

Chignell, Andrew. "Can We Really Vote with Our Forks?: Opportunism and the Threshold Chicken," in *Philosophy Comes to Dinner: Arguments About the Ethics of Eating*, Andrew Chignell, Terence Cuneo, and Matthew C, Halteman, eds. New York: Routledge, 2016.

Chignell, Andrew, Terence Cuneo, and Matthew C, Halteman, eds. *Philosophy Comes to Dinner: Arguments About the Ethics of Eating.* New York: Routledge, 2016.

Christensen, Kimberly. "With Whom Do You Believe Your Lot Is Cast? White Feminists and Racism." *Signs: Journal of Women in Culture and Society* 22, no. 3 (1997).

Clark, Sean. "Organic Farming and Climate Change: The Need for Innovation." *Sustainability* 12, no. 17 (2020).

Cohen, Andrew I., and Christopher H. Wellman, eds. *Contemporary Debates in Applied Ethics*. Malden, Massachusetts: Blackwell Publishing, 2005.

Cohen, Carl. "The Case for the Use of Animals in Biomedical Research." *New England Journal of Medicine* 315, no. 14 (1986).

——. "The Factual Setting of Animal Experimentation," in Carl Cohen and Tom Regan, *The Animal Rights Debate*. Lanham, Maryland: Rowman & Littlefield, 2001.

——. "The Moral Inequality of Species: Why Speciesism Is Right," in Carl Cohen and Tom Regan, *The Animal Rights Debate*. Lanham, Maryland: Rowman & Littlefield, 2001.

——. "Rights and Interests," in Carl Cohen and Tom Regan, *The Animal Rights Debate*. Lanham, Maryland: Rowman & Littlefield, 2001.

Chin, Tina H. T., and Chin-Lon Lin. "Ethical Management of Food Systems: Plant-based Diet as a Holistic Approach." *Asia Pacific Journal of Clinical Nutrition* 18, no. 4 (2009).

Cole, Matthew. "From 'Animal Machines' to 'Happy Meat'? Foucault's Ideas of Disciplinary and Pastoral Power Applied to 'Animal-Centered' Welfare Discourse." *Animals* 1, no. 1 (2011).

Costello, Kimberly, and Gordon Hodson. "Exploring the Roots of Dehumanization: The Role of Human–Animal Similarity in Promoting Immigrant Humanization." *Group Processes and Intergroup Relations* 13, no. 1 (2010).

Craig, W. J., and A, R. Margelis. "Position of the American Dietetic Association: Vegetarian Diets." *Journal of the American Dietetic Association* 109, no. 7 (2009).

Croney, C. C., and R. D. Reynnells. "The Ethics of Semantics: Do We Clarify or Obfuscate Reality to Influence Perceptions of Farm Animal Production?" *Poultry Science* 87, no. 2 (2008).

Das, Ushnik, Anshu Kumari, Shruthi Sharma, and Laxmi T. Rao. "Demonstration of Altruistic Behaviour in Rats." *bioRxiv* 805481 (2019).

de Spinoza, Benedict. *Ethics*, translated by William H. White. New York: Macmillan, 1883.

de Waal, Frans. *Good Natured, The Origins of Right and Wrong in Humans and Other Animals.* Cambridge, Massachusetts: Harvard University Press, 1996.

———. "Morally Evolved: Primate Social Instincts, Human Morality, and the Rise and Fall of 'Veneer Theory,'" in *Primates and Philosophers: How Morality Evolved,* Stephen Macedo and Josiah Ober, eds. Princeton, New Jersey: Princeton University Press, 2006.

———. "The Tower of Morality" in *Primates and Philosophers: How Morality Evolved,* Stephen Macedo and Josiah Ober, eds. Princeton, New Jersey: Princeton University Press, 2006.

———. "Putting the Altruism Back into Altruism: The Evolution of Empathy," *Annual Review of Psychology* 59 (2008).

———. *Are We Smart Enough to Know How Smart Animals Are?* New York: W. W. Norton, 2016.

DeGrazia, David. *Taking Animals Seriously: Mental Life and Moral Status.* Cambridge: Cambridge University Press, 1996.

———. "The Ethics of Confining Animals: From Farms to Zoos to Human Homes," in *The Oxford Handbook of Animal Ethics,* Tom Beauchamp and David DeGrazia, eds. Oxford: Oxford University Press, 2011.

DeGrazia, David, and Tom Beauchamp. "Beyond the 3Rs to a More Comprehensive Framework of Principles for Animal Research Ethics." *ILAR Journal* 60, no. 3 (2019).

Desa, Zalak, and Ying Zhang. "Climate Change and Women's Health: A Scoping Review." *Geohealth* 5, no. 9 (2021).

Descartes, René. Letter to Henry More, 5 February 1649 in *Oeuvres de Descartes* (1903).

Dhont, Kristof, and Gordon Hodson. "Loving and Exploiting Animals: An Introduction," in *Why We Love and Exploit Animals: Bridging Insights from Academia and Advocacy,* Kristof Dhont and Gordon Hodson, eds. New York: Routledge, 2020.

Dhont, Kristof, and Gordon Hodson, eds. *Why We Love and Exploit Animals: Bridging Insights from Academia and Advocacy.* New York: Routledge, 2020.

Dhont, Kristof, Gordon Hodson, and Ana L. Leite. "Common Ideological Roots of Speciesism and Generalized Ethnic Prejudice: The Social Dominance Human–Animal Relations Model (SD-HARM)." *European Journal of Personality* 30, no. 6 (2016).

Dhont, Kristof, Gordon Hodson, Ana C. Leite, and Alina Salmen. "The Psychology of Speciesism," in *Why We Love and Exploit Animals: Bridging Insights from Academia and Advocacy*, Kristof Dhont and Gordon Hodson, eds. New York: Routledge, 2020.

Diener, Ed, Shigehiro Oishi, and Jung Yeun Park. "An Incomplete List of Eminent Psychologists of the Modern Era." *Archives of Scientific Psychology* 2, no. 1 (2014).

Diggles, B. K., S. J. Cooke, J. D. Rose, and W. Sawynok. "Ecology and Welfare of Aquatic Animals in Wild Capture Fisheries." *Reviews in Fish Biology and Fisheries* 21 (2011).

Douglass, Frederick. *Narrative of the Life of Frederick Douglass, an American Slave, Written by Himself.* Boston: Antislavery Office, 1845.

Drimmer, Melvin. "Thoughts on the Persistence of American Racism," *The History Teacher* 4, no. 3 (1970).

Duckitt, John, and Chris G. Sibley. "The Dual Process Motivational Model of Ideology and Prejudice," in *The Cambridge Handbook of the Psychology of Prejudice*, Chris G. Sibley and Fiona Kate Barlow, eds. Cambridge: Cambridge University Press, 2017.

Dugan, Kelly P. "The 'Happy Slave' Narrative and Classics Pedagogy: A Verbal and Visual Analysis of Beginning Greek and Latin Textbooks." *New England Classical Journal* 46, no. 1 (2019).

Dunayer, Joan. "Sexist Words, Speciesist Roots," in *Animals and Women: Feminist Theoretical Explorations*, Carol J. Adams and Josephine Donovan, eds. Durham, North Carolina: Duke University Press, 1995.

——. *Animal Equality: Language and Liberation*. Derwood, Maryland: Ryce Publishing, 2001.

Eliot, Lise. "Brain Development and Physical Aggression: How a Small Gender Difference Grows into a Violence Problem." *Current Anthropology* 62, no. S23 (2021).

Ferrari, Arianna. "Contesting Animal Experiments through Ethics and Epistemology: In Defense of a Political Critique of Animal Experimentation," in *Animal Experimentation: Working Towards a Paradigm Change*, Kathrin Hermann and Kimberley Jayne, eds. Boston: Brill, 2019.

Foer, Jonathan Safran. *Eating Animals*. New York: Back Bay Books, 2009.

——. *We Are the Weather: Saving the Planet Begins at Breakfast*. New York: Farrar, Straus, & Giroux, 2019.

Food and Agriculture Organization of the United Nations. *The State of the World's Fisheries and Aquaculture 2020: Sustainability in Action*. Rome: Food and Agriculture Organization of the United Nations, 2020.

——. *The State of Food Security and Nutrition in the World 2022: Repurposing Food and Agricultural Policies to Make Healthy Diets More Affordable*. Rome: Food and Agriculture Organization of the United Nations, 2022.

Fournier, J., K. Schwean-Lardner, T. D. Knezacek, S. Gomis, and H. L. Classen. "The Effect of Toe Trimming on Behavior, Mobility, Toe Length and Other Indicators of Welfare in Tom Turkeys." *Poultry Science* 94, no. 7 (2015).

Frey, R. G. "Animals and Their Medical Use," in *Contemporary Debates in Applied Ethics*, Andrew I. Cohen and Christopher H. Wellman, eds. Malden, Massachusetts: Blackwell Publishing, 2005.

Friedland, Paul. "Friends for Dinner: The Early Modern Roots of Modern Carnivorous Sensibilities." *History of the Present: A Journal of Critical History* 1, no. 1 (2011).

Friedlander, Henry. *The Origins of Nazi Genocide: From Euthanasia to the Final Solution*. Chapel Hill: University of North Carolina Press, 1995.

Gaarder, Emily. "Where the Boys Aren't: The Predominance of Women in Animal Rights Activism." *Feminist Formations* 23, no. 2 (2011).

Galgut, Elisa. "Raising the Bar in the Justification of Animal Research." *Journal of Animal Ethics* 5, no. 1 (2015).

Garrett, Jeremy R., ed. *The Ethics of Animal Research: Exploring the Controversy*. Cambridge, Massachusetts: MIT Press, 2012.

Gilbert, Martin. *Auschwitz and the Allies*. New York: Holt, Rhinehart, and Winston, 1981.

Gillespie, Kathryn. "How Happy Is Your Meat? (Dis)connectedness in the 'Alternative' Meat Industry." *The Brock Review* 12, no.1 (2011).

Glasser, Carol J. "Tied Oppressions: An Analysis of How Sexist Imagery Reinforces Speciesist Sentiments." *The Brock Review* 12, no.1 (2011).

Glatz, Philip C., and Greg Underwood. "Current Methods and Techniques of Beak Trimming Laying Hens, Welfare Issues and Alternative Approaches." *Animal Production Science* 61, no. 10 (2020).

Glick, Peter, and Susan T. Fiske. "An Ambivalent Alliance: Hostile and Benevolent Sexism as Complementary Justifications for Gender Inequality." *American Psychologist* 56, no. 2 (2001).

Goldhagen, Daniel. *Hitler's Willing Executioners: Ordinary Germans and the Holocaust*. New York: Vintage Books, 1997.

Gordon, Mordechai. "Multicultural Education: Moving Beyond Heroes and Holidays." *Education for Meaning and Social Justice* 17, no. 4 (2004).

Gould, Stephen Jay. "Women's Brains," in *The Panda's Thumb: More Reflections in Natural History*. New York: W. W. Norton, 1980.

Graca, João, Maria Manuela Calheiros, and Abílio Oliveira. "Moral Disengagement in Harmful but Cherished Food Practices? An Exploration into the Case of Meat." *Journal of Agricultural and Environmental Ethics* 27, no. 5 (2014).

Greene, James. "Altruistic Behavior in the Albino Rat." *Psychonomic Science* 14, no. 1 (1969).

Gregory, Neville G. *Animal Welfare and Meat Science*. Wallingford, Oxfordshire: CABI Publishing, 1998.

———. *Animal Welfare and Meat Production*. Wallingford, Oxfordshire: CABI Publishing, 2007.

Griffiths, Roland, R. J. Lamb, Christine A. Sannerud, Nancy A. Ator, and Joseph V. Brady. "Self-injection of Barbituates, Benzodiazepines and Other Sedative-anxiolytics in Baboons." *Psychopharmacology* 103 (1991).

Gutmann, Matthew. "The Animal Inside: Men and Violence." *Current Anthropology* 62, no. S23 (2021).

Harfeld, Jes. "Husbandry to Industry: Animal Agriculture, Ethics and Public Policy." *Between the Species* 10, no. 8 (2010).

Harman, Elizabeth. "The Moral Significance of Animal Pain and Animal Death," in *The Oxford Handbook of Animal Ethics*, Tom Beauchamp and R. G. Frey, eds. Oxford: Oxford University Press, 2011.

Harper, William. "Harper's Memoir on Slavery," in *The Pro-slavery Argument*. Philadelphia: Lippincott, Grambo & Co., 1853.

Harrison, Ruth. *Animal Machines: The New Factory Farming Industry*. Boston: CABI, 2013.

Haynes, Richard P. "The Myth of Happy Meat." *The Philosophy of Food* 39 (2012).

Hegel, Georg Friedrich. *Lectures on the Philosophy of World History*, Johannes Hoffmeister, ed., H. B. Nisbet, trans. Cambridge: Cambridge University Press, 1975.

Hermann, Kathrin, and Kimberley Jayne, eds. *Animal Experimentation: Working Towards a Paradigm Change*. Boston: Leiden, 2019.

Hernandez-Lallement, Julien, Marijn van Wingerden, Sandra Schäble, and Tobias Kalenscher. "Basolateral Amygdala Lesions Abolish Mutual Reward Preferences in Rats." *Neurobiology of Learning and Memory* 127 (2016).

———. "Towards an Animal Model of Callousness." *Neuroscience and Biobehavioral Reviews* 91 (2018).

Hickel, Jason. "Quantifying National Responsibility for Climate Breakdown: An Equality-Based Attribution Approach for Carbon Dioxide Emissions in Excess of the Planetary Boundary." *The Lancet Planetary Health* 4, no. 9 (2020).

Hilberg, Raul. "The Destruction of the European Jews: Dehumanization and Concealment," in *Understanding Prejudice and Discrimination*, Scott Plous, ed. New York: McGraw-Hill, 2003.

Ho, Arnold K., Jim Sidanius, Felicia Pratto, Shana Levin, Lotte Thomsen, Nour Kteily, and Jennifer Sheehy-Skeffington. "Social Dominance Orientation: Revisiting the Structure and Function of a Variable Predicting Social and Political Attitudes." *Personality and Social Psychology Bulletin* 38, no. 5 (2011).

Hodson, Gordon, and Kristof Dhont. "An Integrated Psychology of (Animalistic) Dehumanization Requires a Focus on Human-Animal Relations." *Current Research in Ecological and Social Psychology* 5 (2023).

Hodson, Gordon, Kristof Dhont, and Megan Earle. "Devaluing Animals, 'Animalistic' Humans, and People Who Protect Animals," in *Why We Love and Exploit Animals: Bridging Insights from Academia and Advocacy,* Kristof Dhont and Gordon Hodson, eds. New York: Routledge, 2020.

Holmberg, Tara, and Malin Ideland. "Secrets and Lies: 'Selective Openness' in the Apparatus of Animal Experimentation." *Public Understanding of Science* 21, no.3 (2012).

Hoogland, Carolien, Joop de Boer, and Jan Boersema. "Transparency of the Meat Chain in the Light of Food Culture and History." *Appetite* 45, no. 1 (2005).

Höss, Rudolf. *Death Dealer: The Memoirs of the SS Kommandant at Auschwitz*, Andrew Pollinger, trans. New York: Worth Publishers, 1996.

Hume, David. *The Philosophical Works of David Hume,* volume II, T. H. Green and T. H. Grose, eds. London: Longmans, Green & Co., 1882.

Hyers Lauri. "Myths Used to Legitimize the Exploitation of Animals: An Application of Social Dominance Theory." *Anthrozoös* 19, no. 3 (2006).

Iacobbo, K., and M. Iacobbo. *Vegetarians and Vegans in America Today.* Westport, Connecticut: Greenwood Publishing Group, 2006.

Imhoff, Daniel. "Myth: Industrial Food Benefits the Environment and Wildlife" in *The CAFO Reader: The Tragedy of Industrial Animal Factories,* Daniel Imhoff, ed. Berkeley, California, Watershed Media, 2010.

——, ed. *The CAFO Reader: The Tragedy of Industrial Animal Factories.* Berkeley, California, Watershed Media, 2010.

Jackson, Lynne M. *The Psychology of Prejudice: From Attitudes to Social Action*, 2nd ed. Washington, D.C.: American Psychological Association, 2020.

Jackson, Lynne M. and Aaron Gibbings. "Social Dominance and Legitimizing Myths About Animal Use." *Anthrozoös* 29, no. 1 (2015).

Joy, Melanie. *Why We Love Dogs, Eat Pigs and Wear Cows: An Introduction to Carnism.* San Francisco: Conari Press, 2010.

Kagan, Shelly. "What's Wrong with Speciesism?" *Journal of Applied Philosophy* 33, no. 1 (2016).

Kalechofsky, Roberta. "Dedicated to Descartes' Niece: The Women's Movement in the Nineteenth Century and Anti-Vivisection." *Between the Species* 8, no. 2 (1992).

Kellogg, Kathy, and Bob Kellogg. *Raising Pigs Successfully.* Charlotte, Vermont: Williamson, 1985.

Kenehan, Sarah. "The Moral Status of Animal Research Subjects in Industry: A Stakeholder Analysis," in *Animal Experimentation: Working Towards a Paradigm Change*, Kathrin Hermann and Kimberley Jayne, eds. Boston: Leiden, 2019.

Klugman, Jeni, and Beatrice Duncan. "Shaping the Law for Women and Girls: Experiences and Lessons from UN Women's Interventions 2015–2020." U.N. Women (2022).

Knight, Sara, and Louise Barnett. "Justifying Attitudes Toward Animal Use: A Qualitative Study of People's Views and Beliefs." *Anthrozoös* 21, no. 1 (2008).

Kok, Bjorn, Wesley Malcorps, Michael F. Tlusty, Mahmoud M. Eltholth, Neil A. Auchterlonie, David C. Little, Robert Harmsen, et. al. "Fish as Feed: Using Economic Allocation to Quantify the Fish In: Fish Out Ratio of Major Fed Aquaculture Species." *Aquaculture* 528 (2020).

Korsgaard, Christine. *Fellow Creatures: Our Obligations to Other Animals.* Oxford: Oxford University Press, 2018.

Krings, Victoria, Kristof Dhont, and Alina Salmen, "The Moral Divide Between High- and Low-Status Animals: The Role of Human Supremacy Beliefs." *Anthrozoös* 34, no. 6 (2021).

Kteily, Nour, Arnold K. Ho, and Jim Sidanius. "Hierarchy in the Mind: The Predictive Power of Social Dominance Orientation across Social Contexts and Domains." *Journal of Experimental Social Psychology* 48, no. 2 (2012).

Kteily, Nour, and Jennifer A. Richardson. "Perceiving the World through Hierarchy-shaped Glasses: On the Need to Embed Social Identity Effects on Macro-level Social Inequality and Violence across Societies." *Psychological Inquiry* 27, no. 4 (2016).

LaFollette, Hugh, and William Aiken, eds. *World Hunger and Moral Obligation.* Englewood Cliffs, New Jersey: Prentice-Hall, 1977.

Lawrence, Elizabeth. "Conflicting Ideologies: Views of Animal Rights Opponents and Their Advocates." *Society and Animals* 2, no. 2 (1994).

Langford, Dale, Sara E. Crager, Zarrar Shehzad, Shad B. Smith, Susana G. Sotocinal, Jeremy S. Levenstadt, Mona Lisa Chanda, et al. "Social Modulation of Pain as Evidence for Empathy in Mice." *Science* 312, no. 5782 (2006).

Lederer, Susan. "Political Animals: The Shaping of Biomedical Research Literature in Twentieth-Century America." *Isis* 83, no. 1 (1992).

Leitzman, Claus. "Nutrition Ecology: The Contribution of Vegetarian Diets." *American Journal of Clinical Nutrition* 78, no. 3 (Supplement) (2003).

Levi, Primo. *The Drowned and the Saved.* London: Joseph, 1988.

Lifton, Robert Jay. *The Nazi Doctors: Medical Killing and the Psychology of Genocide.* New York: Basic Books, 1986.

Lopez, Donna. "A Goat Named Kevin." *Dairy Goat Guide* (March, 1984).

Loughnan, Steve, Brock Bastian, and Nick Haslam. "The Psychology of Eating Animals." *Current Directions in Psychological Science* 23, no. 2 (2014).

Loughnan, Steve, Nick Haslam, and Brock Bastian. "The Role of Meat Consumption in the Denial of Moral Status and Mind to Meat Animals." *Appetite* 55, no. 1 (2010).

Luke, Brian. *Brutal: Manhood and the Exploitation of Animals.* Urbana: University of Illinois Press, 2007.

MacClancy, Jeremy. *Consuming Culture: Why You Eat What You Eat.* New York: Henry Holt, 1992.

Macedo, Stephen, and Josiah Ober, eds. *Primates and Philosophers: How Morality Evolved.* Princeton, New Jersey: Princeton University Press, 2006.

MacInnis, Cara C., and Gordon Hodson, "It Ain't Easy Eating Greens: Evidence of Bias toward Vegetarians and Vegans from Both Source and Target." *Group Processes and Intergroup Relations* 20, no. 6 (2016).

MacKinnon, Catharine A. "Difference and Dominance: On Sex Discrimination," in *Feminism and Politics*, Anne Phillips, ed. Oxford: Oxford University Press, 1998.

——. "Of Mice and Men: A Feminist Fragment on Animal Rights," in *Animal Rights: Current Debates and New Directions*, Cass R. Sunstein and Martha C. Nussbaum, eds. Oxford: Oxford University Press, 2004.

Maher, Jennifer, Harriet Pierpont, and Piers Beirne, eds. *The Palgrave International Handbook of Animal Abuse Studies.* London: Palgrave Macmillan, 2017.

Marcus, Erik. *Meat Market: Animals, Ethics, & Money.* Boston: Brio Press, 2005.

Mares, Marie-Louise, and Zhongdang Pan. "Effects of *Sesame Street*: A Meta-analysis of Children's Learning in 15 Countries." *Journal of Applied Developmental Psychology* 34, no. 3 (2013).

Marsh, Peter. *The Supremacist Syndrome: How Domination Underpins Slavery, Genocide, the Exploitation of Women and the Maltreatment of Animals.* Brooklyn, New York: Lantern Publishing and Media, 2021.

Mason, Jim, and Peter Singer. *Animal Factories: What Agribusiness Is Doing to the Family Farm, the Environment, and Your Health.* New York: Harmony Books, 1990.

Masserman, Jules H., Stanley Wechkin, and William Terris. "'Altruistic' Behavior in Rhesus Monkeys." *American Journal of Psychiatry* 121, no. 6 (1964).

McFarland, Sam. "Authoritarianism, Social Dominance, and Other Roots of Generalized Prejudice." *Political Psychology* 31, no. 3 (2010).

McMullen, Steven. *Animals and the Economy.* London: Palgrave Macmillan, 2016.

Mebane, Minou Ella, Antonio Aiello, and Donata Francescato. "Political Gender Gap and Social Dominance Orientation," in *Psycho-social Aspects of Human Sexuality and Ethics*, Dhastagir Sheriff, ed. London: IntechOpen, 2020.

Melina, Vesanto, Winston Craig, and Susan Levin. "Position of the Academy of Nutrition and Dietetics: Vegetarian Diets." *Journal of the Academy of Nutrition and Dietetics* 116, no. 12 (2016).

Meltzer, Milton. *Slavery: A World History*. New York: Da Capo Press, 1993.

Meyza, K. Z, I. Ben-Ami Bartal, M. H. Monfils, J. B. Panksepp, and E. Knapska. "The Roots of Empathy: Through the Lens of Rodent Model." *Neuroscience & Biobehavioral Reviews* 76 (2017).

Miele, Mara. "The Taste of Happiness: Free Range Chicken." *Environment and Planning A* 43, no. 9 (2011).

Milfont, Taciano Lemos, Paul G. Bain, Yoshihisa Kashima, Victor Corral-Verdugo, Carlota Pasquali, Lars-Olof Johansson, Yanjun Guan, Valdiney V. Gouveia, et. al. "On the Relation between Social Dominance Orientation and Environmentalism: A 25-Nation Study." *Social Psychological and Personality Science* 9, no. 7 (2018).

Milfont, Taciano Lemos, Isabel Richter, Chris G. Sibley, Marc S. Wilson, and Ronald Fischer. "Environmental Consequences of the Desire to Dominate and Be Superior." *Personality and Social Psychology Bulletin* 39, no. 9 (2013).

Miller, A. G., ed. *The Social Psychology of Good and Evil*. New York: Guilford Press, 2004.

Minson, Julia, and Benoit Monin. "Do-Gooder Derogation: Disparaging Morally Motivated Minorities to Defuse Anticipated Reproach." *Social Psychological and Personality Science* 3, no. 2 (2012).

Minter, Frank. *The Politically Incorrect Guide to Hunting*. Washington, D.C.: Regnery Publishing, 2007.

Mitchell, Les. "Moral Disengagement and Support for Nonhuman Animal Farming." *Society & Animals* 19 (2011).

Morrison, Adrian. "Making Choices in the Laboratory," in *Why Animal Experimentation Matters: The Use of Animals in Medical Research*, Ellen Frankel Paul and Jeffrey Paul, eds. New Brunswick, New Jersey: Transaction Publishers, 2001.

Murray, Fiona. "The Oncomouse That Roared: Hybrid Exchange Strategies as a Source of Distinction at the Boundary of Overlapping Institutions." *Daedalus* 131, no. 2 (2002).

Nibert, David. *Animal Rights/Human Rights: Entanglements of Oppression and Liberation*. Boulder, Colorado: Rowman and Littlefield, 2002.

Nobis, Nathan. "Carl Cohen's 'Kind' Arguments *For* Animal Rights and *Against* Human Rights." *Journal of Applied Philosophy* 21, no. 1 (2004).

Norvell, Kim. "Iowa farm forced to euthanize pigs was 'infiltrated' by animal activists." *Des Moines Register* (May 20, 2020).

Nuffield Council on Bioethics. *The Ethics of Research Involving Animals: The Report of the Nuffield Council on Bioethics*. London: Nuffield Council on Bioethics, 2005.

Nussbaum, Martha. *Justice for Animals: Our Collective Responsibility*. New York: Simon & Schuster, 2022.

Orwell, George. "Politics and the English Language." *Horizon* 13, no. 76 (1946).

Paciello, Marinella, Roberta Fida, Carlo Tramontano, Catia Lupinetti, and Gian Vittorio Caprara. "Stability and Change of Moral Disengagement and Its Impact on Aggression and Violence in Late Adolescence." *Child Development* 79 no. 5 (2008).

Paul, Elizabeth. "Us and Them: Scientists' and Animal Rights Campaigners' Views of the Animal Experimentation Debate." *Society and Animals* 3, no. 1 (1995).

Paul, Ellen Frankel, and Jeffrey Paul, eds. *Why Animal Experimentation Matters: The Use of Animals in Medical Research*. New Brunswick, New Jersey: Transaction Publishers, 2001.

Pelletier, Nathan, Rich Pirog, and Rebecca Rasmussen. "Comparative Life-cycle and Environmental Impacts of Three Beef Production Strategies in the Upper Midwestern United States." *Agricultural Systems* 103 (2010).

Pérez-Manrique, Ana, and Antoni Gomila. "The Comparative Study of Empathy: Sympathetic Concern and Empathic Perspective-taking in Non-human Animals." *Biological Reviews* 93, no.1 (2017).

Pettigrew, Thomas F., and Linda R. Tropp. "A Meta-Analytic Test of Intergroup Contact Theory." *Journal of Personality and Social Psychology* 90, no. 5 (2006).

Phillips, Mary. *Constructing Laboratory Animals: An Ethnographic Study in the Sociology of Science.* New York, New York University Press, 1991.

Piazza, Jared. "People Love Animals Yet Continue to Eat Them," in *Why We Love and Exploit Animals*, Kristof Dhont and Gordon Hodson, eds. New York: Routledge, 2020.

Piazza, Jared, and Steve Loughnan. "When Meat Gets Personal, Animals' Minds Matter Less: Motivated Use of Intelligence Information in Judgments of Moral Standing." *Social Psychological and Personality Science* 7, no. 8 (2016).

Piazza, Jared, Matthew B. Ruby, Steve Loughnan, Mischel Luong, Juliana Kulik, Hanne M. Watkins, and Mirra Seigerman. "Rationalizing Meat Consumption: The 4Ns." *Appetite* 91 (2015).

Pierce, Jessica. "Putting the 'Free' Back in Freedom: The Failure and Future of Animal Welfare Science," in *Why We Love and Exploit Animals*, Kristof Dhont and Gordon Hodson, eds. New York: Routledge, 2020.

Pimentel, David, and Marcia Pimentel. "Sustainability of Meat-based and Plant-based Diets and the Environment." *American Journal of Clinical Nutrition* 78, no. 3 (2003).

Plous, Scott, and Harold Herzog, "Reliability of Protocol Reviews for Animal Research." *Science* 293, no. 5530 (2001).

Plous, Scott. "Is There Such a Thing as Prejudice Toward Animals?" in *Understanding Prejudice and Discrimination*, Scott Plous, ed. New York: McGraw-Hill, 2003.

Plous, Scott, ed. *Understanding Prejudice and Discrimination.* New York: McGraw-Hill, 2003.

Pollan, Michael. "An Animal's Place," *New York Times Magazine* (November 10, 2002).

——. *The Omnivore's Dilemma: A Natural History of Four Meals.* New York: Penguin Press, 2006.

Poore, J. and T. Nemecek. "Reducing Food's Environmental Impacts through Producers and Consumers." *Science* 363, no. 6392 (2018).

Pratto, Felicia, James H. Liu, Shana Levin, Jim Sidanius, Margaret Shih, Hagit Bachrach, and Peter Hegarty. "Social Dominance Orientation and the Legitimization of Inequality Across Cultures." *Journal of Cross-Cultural Psychology* 31, no. 3 (2000).

Pratto, Felicia, James Sidanius, Lisa M. Stallworth, and Bertram F. Malle. "Social Dominance Orientation: A Personality Variable Predicting Social and Political Attitudes." *Journal of Personality and Social Psychology* 67, no. 4 (1994).

Rachels, James. *Created from Animals: The Moral Implications of Darwinism*. Oxford: Oxford University Press, 1990.

——. "Vegetarianism and 'The Other Weight Problem,'" in *World Hunger and Moral Obligation*, Hugh LaFollette and William Aiken, eds. Englewood Cliffs, New Jersey: Prentice-Hall, 1977.

Ramsey, Patricia G. "Multicultural Education for Young Children," in *The Routledge International Companion to Multicultural Education*, James A. Banks, ed. New York: Routledge, 2009.

Rechtschaffen, Allan, Bernard M. Bergmann, Carol A. Everson, Clete A. Kushida, and Marcia A. Gilliland. "Sleep Deprivation in the Rat: X. Integration and Discussion of the Findings." *Sleep* 12, no.1 (1989).

Reijnders, Lucas, and Sam Soret. "Quantification of the Environmental Impact of Different Dietary Protein Choices." *American Journal of Clinical Nutrition* 78 (supplement) (2003).

Robb, D. H. F., and S. C. Kestin. "Methods to Kill Fish: Field Observations and Literature Reviewed." *Animal Welfare* 11 (2002).

Robbins, John. *Diet for a New America: How Your Food Choices Affect Your Health, Your Happiness, and the Future of Life on Earth*. Tiburon, California: H. J. Kramer, 2012.

——. *No Happy Cows: Dispatches from the Frontlines of the Food Revolution*. San Francisco: Conari Press, 2012.

Robnett, Belinda. "African-American Women in the Civil Rights Movement, 1954–1965: Gender, Leadership, and Micromobilization." *American Journal of Sociology* 101, no. 6 (1996).

Rojas-Soto, Michelle. "Oppression Without Hierarchy: Racial Justice and Animal Advocacy," in *Antiracism in Animal Advocacy: Igniting Cultural Transformation*, Jasmin Singer, ed. Brooklyn: Lantern Publishing & Media, 2021.

Rothgerber, Hank. "Efforts to Overcome Vegetarian-induced Dissonance among Meat Eaters," *Appetite* 79 (2014).

——. "How We Love and Hurt Animals: Considering Cognitive Dissonance in Young Meat Eaters," in *Why We Love and Exploit Animals: Bridging Insights from Academia and Advocacy*, Kristof Dhont and Gordon Hodson, eds. New York: Routledge, 2020.

Rous, F. Peyton. "Points to Look Out for in Connection with the Antivivisectionists."

Ruini, Luca Fernando, Roberto Ciati, Carlo Alberto Pratesi, Massimo Marino, Ludovica Principato, and Eleonora Vannuzzi. "Working Toward Healthy and Sustainable Diets: The 'Double Pyramid Model' Developed by the Barilla Center for Food and Nutrition to Raise Awareness about the Environmental and Nutritional Impact of Foods." *Frontiers in Nutrition*, 2, no. 9 (2015).

Rush, Benjamin. "Observations Intended to Favour Supposition that the Black Color (as it is called) of the Negroes is derived from the Leprosy." *Transactions of the American Philosophical Society* 4 (1799).

Russell, W. M. S., and R. L. Burch. *The Principles of Humane Experimental Technique*. London: Methuen, 1959.

Rutland, Adam, Lindsey Cameron, Laura Bennett, and Jennifer Ferrell. "Interracial Contact and Racial Constancy: A Multi-site Study of Racial Intergroup Bias in 3-5-year-old Anglo-British Children." *Applied Developmental Psychology* 26 no. 6 (2005).

Ryder, Richard. "Speciesism," in *Encyclopedia of Animal Rights and Animal Welfare*, Marc Bekoff and Carron Meaney, eds. Chicago: Fitzroy Dearborn, 1998.

Sabaté, Joan. "The Contribution of Vegetarian Diets to Health and Disease: A Paradigm Shift," *American Journal of Clinical Nutrition* 78 (supp.) (2003).

Sagan, Carl, and Ann Druyan. *Shadows of Forgotten Ancestors: A Search for Who We Are*. New York: Random House, 1992.

Salmen, Alina, and Gordon Hodson, "Animalizing Women and Feminizing (Vegan) Men: The Psychological Intersections of Sexism, Speciesism, Meat, and Masculinity." *Social and Personality Psychology Compass* 17, no. 2 (2023).

Sapontzis, S. F. "The Moral Significance of Interests," *Environmental Ethics* 4, no. 4 (1982).

——. *Morals, Reason, and Animals*. Philadelphia: Temple University Press, 1987.

Schüßler, Charlotte, Susanne Nicola, Susanne Stoll-Kleemann, and Bartosz Bartkowski. "Moral Disengagement in the Media Discourses on Meat and Dairy Production Systems." *Appetite* 196, no. 107269 (2024).

Serpell, James. *In the Company of Animals: A Study of Human–Animal Relationships*. Cambridge: Cambridge University Press, 1996.

Sibley, Chris G., and Fiona Kate Barlow. "An Introduction to the Psychology of Prejudice," in *The Cambridge Handbook of The Psychology of Prejudice*, Chris G. Sibley and Fiona Kate Barlow, eds. Cambridge: Cambridge University Press, 2017.

——, eds. *The Cambridge Handbook of The Psychology of Prejudice*. Cambridge: Cambridge University Press, 2017.

Sidanius, Jim, B. J. Cling, and Felicia Pratto. "Ranking and Linking as a Function of Sex and Gender Role Attitudes." *Journal of Social Issues* 47 no. 3 (1991).

Sidanius, Jim, and Felicia Pratto. *Social Dominance: An Intergroup Theory of Social Hierarchy and Oppression*. Cambridge: Cambridge University Press, 1999.

Simms, W. Gilmore. "The Morals of Slavery," in *The Pro-Slavery Argument*. Philadelphia: Lippincott & Grambo, 1853.

Singer, Peter. *Ethics into Action: Henry Spira and the Animal Rights Movement*. Lanham, Maryland: Rowman & Littlefield, 1998.

——. *Animal Liberation*. New York: HarperCollins, 2009.

Singer, Peter, and Jim Mason, *The Ethics of What We Eat: Why Our Food Choices Matter*. New York: Rodale, 2007.

Sivaselvachandran, Sivaani, Erinn L. Acland, Salsabil Abdallah, and Loren J. Martin. "Behavioral and Mechanistic Insight into Rodent Empathy." *Neuroscience and Biobehavioral Reviews* 91 (2018).

Smith, David Livingstone. *Less Than Human: Why We Demean, Enslave, and Exterminate Others*. New York: St. Martin's Press, 2011.

——. "Paradoxes of Dehumanization," *Social Theory and Practice* 42, no. 2 (2016).

Smith, Wesley. *A Rat Is a Pig Is a Dog Is a Boy: The Human Cost of the Animal Rights Movement*. New York: Encounter Books, 2010.

Spiegel, Marjorie. *The Dreaded Comparison: Human and Animal Slavery.* New York: Mirror Books, 1996.

Steinfeld, Henning, Pierre Gerber, Tom D. Wassenaar, Vincent Castel, and Cees De Haan. *Livestock's Long Shadow: Environmental Issues and Options.* Rome: Food and Agriculture Organization of the United Nations (2006).

Stephan, Cookie White, Lausanne Renfro, and Walter G. Stephan. "The Evaluation of Multicultural Education Programs: Techniques and a Meta-Analysis," in *Education Programs for Improving Intergroup Relations*, Walter G. Stephan and W. Paul Vogt, eds. New York: Teachers College Press, 2004.

Stephan, Walter G., and W. Paul Vogt, eds. *Education Programs for Improving Intergroup Relations.* New York: Teachers College Press, 2004.

Stier, Ken, and Emmett Hopkins. "Floating Hog Farms," in *The CAFO Reader: The Tragedy of Industrial Animal Factories*, Daniel Imhoff, ed. Berkeley, California: Watershed Media, 2010.

Stucki, Saskia. "(Certified) Humane Violence? Animal Welfare Labels, the Ambivalence of Humanizing the Inhumane, and What International Humanitarian Law Has to Do with It." *American Journal of International Law* 111 (2017).

Sunstein, Cass R., and Martha C. Nussbaum, eds. *Animal Rights: Current Debates and New Directions.* Oxford: Oxford University Press, 2004.

Swan, James. *In Defense of Hunting.* New York: HarperCollins, 1985.

Syropoulos, Stylianos, Uri Lifshin, Jeff Greenberg, Dylan E. Horner, and Bernhard Leidner. "Bigotry and the Human–Animal Divide: (Dis)Belief in Human Evolution and Bigoted Attitudes Across Different Cultures." *Journal of Personality and Social Psychology* 123, no. 6 (2022).

Sztybel, David. "Can the Treatment of Animals Be Compared to the Holocaust?" *Ethics and the Environment* 11, no. 1 (2006).

Tannenbaum, Jerrold. "The Paradigm Shift toward Animal Happiness: What It Is, Why It Is Happening, and What It Portends for Medical Research," in *Why Animal Experimentation Matters: The Use of Animals in Medical Research*, Ellen Frankel Paul and Jeffrey Paul, eds. New Brunswick, New Jersey: Transaction Publishers, 2001.

Taylor, Dorceta E. "Gender and Racial Diversity in Environmental Organizations: Uneven Accomplishments and Cause for Concern." *Environmental Justice* 8, no. 5 (2015).

Taylor, L. J. *National Hog Farmer* (March, 1978).

Taylor, N., and H. Fraser, "Slaughterhouses: The Language of Life, the Discourse of Death," in *The Palgrave International Handbook of Animal Abuse Studies*, Jennifer Maher, Harriet Pierpont, and Piers Beirne, eds. London: Palgrave Macmillan, 2017.

te Velde, Hein, Noelle Aarts, and Cees van Woerkum. "Dealing with Ambivalence: Farmers' and Consumers' Perceptions of Animal Welfare in Livestock Breeding." *Journal of Agricultural and Environmental Ethics* 15, no. 2 (2002).

Thiault, Lauric, Camilo Mora, Joshua E. Cinner, William W. L. Cheung, Nicholas A. J. Graham, Fraser A. Januchowski-Hartley, David Mouillot, et al. "Escaping the Perfect Storm of Simultaneous Climate Change Impacts on Agriculture and Marine Fisheries." *Science Advances* 5, no. 11 (2019).

Thomas, Keith. *Man and the Natural World: Changing Attitudes in England 1500–1800.* Oxford: Oxford University Press, 1983.

Tsai, Ling-Ling, Bernard M. Bergmann, and Allan Rechtschaffen. "Sleep Deprivation in the Rat: XVI. Effects in a Light-Dark Cycle," *Sleep* 15, no. 6 (1992).

Tulogdi, Áron, Máté Tóth, Beáta Barsvári, László Biró, Éva Mikics, and József Haller. "Effects of Resocialization on Post-Weaning Social Isolation-Induced Abnormal Aggression and Social Deficits in Rats." *Developmental Psychobiology* 56, no. 1 (2014).

Uenal, Faith, Jim Sidanius, and Sander van der Linden. "Social and Ecological Dominance: Two Sides of the Same Coin? Social and Ecological Dominance Orientations Predict Decreased Support for Climate Change Mitigation Policies." *Group Processes and Intergroup Relations* 25 no. 6 (2022).

Uenal, Faith, Jim Sidanius, Rakoen Maertens1, Sa-Kiera T.J. Hudson, Gregory Davis, and Asma Ghani. "The Roots of Ecological Dominance Orientation: Assessing Individual Preferences for an

Anthropocentric and Hierarchically Organized World." *Journal of Environmental Psychology* 81 (2022).

Ueno, Hiroshi, Shunsuke Suemitsu, Shinji Murakami, Naoya Kitamura, Kenta Wani, Motoi Okamoto, Yosuke Matsumoto, et al. "Empathic Behavior According to the State of Others in Mice." *Brain and Behavior* 8, no. 7 (2018).

Velasquez, Manuel, Claire Andre, Thomas Shanks, and Michael J. Meyer. "Justice and Fairness." *Issues in Ethics* 3, no. 2 (1990).

Vermeulen, Sonia J., Bruce M. Campbell, and John S. I. Ingram. "Climate Change and Food Systems." *Annual Review of Environment and Resources* 37, no. 1 (2012).

Višak, Tatjana. *Killing Happy Animals: Explorations in Utilitarian Ethics*. New York: Palgrave Macmillan, 2013.

Waller, James. *Becoming Evil: How Ordinary People Commit Genocide and Mass Killing*, 2nd ed. Oxford: Oxford University Press, 2007.

Warren, Karen. "The Power and Promise of Ecological Feminism," *Environmental Ethics* 12, no. 2 (1990).

Wechkin, Stanley, Jules Masserman, and William Terris, Jr. "Shock to a Conspecific as an Aversive Stimulus." *Psychonomic Science* 1, no. 1 (1964).

Wegner, Rhiana, Antonia Abbey, and Jacqueline Woerner. "Sexual Assault Perpetrators' Justifications for Their Actions: Relationships to Rape Supportive Attitudes, Incident Characteristics, and Future Perpetration." *Violence Against Women* 21, no. 8 (2015).

Weary, Daniel, Lee Niel, Frances C. Flower, and David Fraser. "Identifying and Preventing Pain in Animals." *Applied Animal Behavior Science* 100, no. 1 (2006).

Webster, John. *Animal Welfare: A Cool Eye Towards Eden*. Oxford: Blackwell Publishing, 1994.

Weisensel, Russell. *Vealer USA* (July/August 1982).

West, Pru Hobson, and Ashley Davies. "Societal Sentience: Construction of the Public in Animal Research Policy and Practice." *Science, Technology, and Human Values* 43, no. 4 (2018).

White, Robert. "Antivivisection: The Reluctant Hydra." *The American Scholar* 40, no. 3 (1971).

Whiten, Andrew. "The Burgeoning Reach of Animal Culture." *Science* 372, no. 6537 (2021).

Williams, John, Deborah Best, and Donna Boswell. "The Measurement of Children's Racial Attitudes in the Early School Years." *Child Development* 46 (1975).

Wolfson, David. "Beyond the Law: Agribusiness and the Systemic Abuse of Animals." *Lewis and Clark Animal Law Review* 2 Animal L 123 (1996).

Working Group of the Oxford Centre for Animal Ethics. *Normalizing the Unthinkable: The Ethics of Using Animals in Research*, Andrew Linzey and Clair Linzey, eds. Oxford: Oxford Centre for Animal Ethics, 2015.

Working Party of the Institute of Medical Ethics. *Lives in the Balance: The Ethics of Using Animals in Biomedical Research*, Jane A. Smith and Kenneth M. Boyd, eds. Oxford: Oxford University Press, 1991.

Wrangham, Richard, and Dale Peterson. *Demonic Males: Apes and the Origins of Human Violence*. Boston: Houghton Mifflin, 1996.

Wright, Stephen C., Arthur Aron, Tracy McLaughlin-Volpe, and Stacy A. Ropp. "The Extended Contact Effect: Knowledge of Cross-Group Friendships and Prejudice." *Journal of Personality and Social Psychology* 73, no. 1 (1997).

Zimbardo, Philip G. "A Situationist Perspective on the Psychology of Evil: Understanding How Good People Are Transformed into Perpetrators." in *The Social Psychology of Good and Evil*, A. G. Miller, ed. New York: Guilford Press, 2004.

Notes

Introduction

1 Depending on the context, in this book non-human animals will sometimes be referred to simply as *animals* to increase readability. The book will also discuss how our need to see humans as qualitatively different from other animals is so strong that we have revised the definition of the word *animal* to exclude humans.
2 Michael Pollan, *The Omnivore's Dilemma: A Natural History of Four Meals* (New York: Penguin Press, 2006), 313.
3 Ibid., 323, 320.
4 *Understanding Prejudice and Discrimination*, edited by Scott Plous (New York: McGraw-Hill, 2003), 131; 234.
5 Ibid., 131–132, 234.
6 Pollan, *The Omnivore's Dilemma,* 310.
7 Moral philosophers sometimes refer to the argument that everything found in nature is good as the *naturalistic fallacy*.
8 Pollan, *The Omnivore's Dilemma,* 320.
9 See Tatjana Višak, *Killing Happy Animals: Explorations in Utilitarian Ethics* (New York: Palgrave Macmillan, 2013), 12.
10 Pollan, *The Omnivore's Dilemma*, 320, 362.
11 Ibid., 231–232.
12 Albert Bandura, *Moral Disengagement: How People Do Harm and Live with Themselves* (New York: Worth Publishers, 2016), 48–53, 56–58, 64–69, and 84–89.

13 Bandura's theory of moral disengagement has been so productive that his work has been cited by others more than 200,000 times, far more than any other psychologist of modern times. Ed Diener, Shigehiro Oishi, and Jung Yeun Park, "An Incomplete List of Eminent Psychologists of the Modern Era," *Archives of Scientific Psychology* 2 (1) (2014), 24.

14 Kristof Dhont and Gordon Hodson, "Loving and Exploiting Animals: An Introduction," in *Why We Love and Exploit Animals: Bridging Insights from Academia and Advocacy*, edited by Kristof Dhont and Gordon Hodson (New York: Routledge, 2020), 1–2.

15 Saskia Stucki, "(Certified) Humane Violence? Animal Welfare Labels, the Ambivalence of Humanizing the Inhumane, and What International Humanitarian Law Has to Do with It," *American Journal of International Law* 111 (2017), 280.

16 Carl Cohen, "The Case for the Use of Animals in Biomedical Research," *New England Journal of Medicine* 315 (14) (1986), 866.

17 Christopher Browning, *Ordinary Men: Reserve Battalion 101 and the Final Solution in Poland* (New York: Harper Collins, 2017), 73.

18 Ibid., 59.

19 Ibid., 87.

Chapter 1: The Exonerative Use of Language

1 Henry Friedlander, *The Origins of Nazi Genocide: From Euthanasia to the Final Solution* (Chapel Hill: University of North Carolina Press, 1995), 109.

2 Ibid., 74.

3 Melanie Joy, *Why We Love Dogs, Eat Pigs and Wear Cows: An Introduction to Carnism* (San Francisco: Conari Press, 2010), 48; Robert Berg and David Halvorson, *Turkey Management Guide* (St. Paul, Minnesota: Turkey Growers Association, 1985), 19; quoted in Joan Dunayer, *Animal Equality: Language and Liberation* (Derwood, Maryland: Ryce Publishing, 2001), 130.

4 Sometimes this use of euphemisms is intentional. In an editorial entitled "Let's Kill Slaughtering," a meat industry journal once advised readers to call places where animals are slaughtered a *meat plant* or a

meat factory, not a *slaughterhouse*. Dunayer, *Animal Equality*, 137; cited in Les Mitchell, "Moral Disengagement and Support for Nonhuman Animal Farming," *Society & Animals* 19 (2011), 50.

5   Donna Lopez "A Goat Named Kevin," *Dairy Goat Guide,* March 1984, 19; quoted in Dunayer, *Animal Equality*, 139.

6   As Bandura noted, activities can take on very different appearances depending on what they are called. Albert Bandura, "Moral Disengagement in the Perpetration of Inhumanities," *Personality and Social Psychology Review* 3 (3) (1999), 195.

7   Roland Griffiths et al., "Self-injection of Barbituates, Benzodiazepines and Other Sedative-anxiolytics in Baboons," *Psychopharmacology* 103 (1991), 154–161.

8   Ling-Ling Tsai, Bernard M. Bergmann, and Allan Rechtschaffen, "Sleep Deprivation in the Rat: XVI. Effects in a Light-Dark Cycle," *Sleep* 15 (6) (1992), 538; cited in Dunayer, *Animal Equality,* 111.

9   Allan Rechtschaffen et al., "Sleep Deprivation in the Rat: X. Integration and Discussion of the Findings," *Sleep* 12 (1), 69.

10 Raul Hilberg, "The Destruction of the European Jews: Dehumanization and Concealment," in *Understanding Prejudice and Discrimination*, edited by Scott Plous (New York: McGraw-Hill, 2003), 283–284.

11 Arnold Arluke, "Trapped in a Guilt Cage," *New Scientist* 134 (1815) (1992), 35.

12 Dunayer, *Animal Equality*, 111.

13 Kathryn Gillespie, "How Happy Is Your Meat? (Dis)connectedness in the 'Alternative' Meat Industry," *The Brock Review* 12 (1) (2011), 113.

14 James Serpell, *In the Company of Animals: A Study of Human–Animal Relationships* (Cambridge: Cambridge University Press, 1996), 197.

15 *AVMA Guidelines for the Euthanasia of Animals: 2020 Edition* (Schaumburg, Illinois: American Veterinary Medical Association, 2020), 6.

16 Angela Baysinger et al., "A Case Study of Ventilation Shutdown with the Addition of High Temperature and Humidity for Depopulation of Pigs," *Journal of the American Veterinary Medical Association* 259 (4), 420.

17 Kim Norvell, "Iowa Farm Forced to Euthanize Pigs Was 'Infiltrated' by Animal Activists," *Des Moines Register* May 20, 2020, accessed

on March 22, 2022, at https://www.desmoinesregister.com/story/news/2020/05/20/iowa-farm-forced-euthanize-pigs-infiltrated-animal-activists/5232631002/.

18 Meat producers have also killed several million chickens and turkeys using similar methods of ventilation shutdown, which were described as "a humane depopulation method" by a spokesperson for Poultry World, a poultry industry trade organization. Accessed on May 22, 2022 at https://www.poultryworld.net/health-nutrition/ventilation-shutdown-a-humane-depopulation-method/.

19 George Orwell, "Politics and the English Language," *Horizon* 13 (76) (1946), 261–262.

20 Susan Lederer, "Political Animals: The Shaping of Biomedical Research Literature in Twentieth-Century America," *Isis* 83 (1) (1992), 70; Scott Plous, "Is There Such a Thing as Prejudice Toward Animals," in *Understanding Prejudice and Discrimination*, edited by Scott Plous (New York: McGraw-Hill, 2003), 514.

21 Orwell, "Politics and the English Language," 262.

Chapter 2: Negate the Harm

1 Rudolf Höss, *Death Dealer: The Memoirs of the SS Kommandant at Auschwitz*, translated by Andrew Pollinger (New York: Worth Publishers, 1996), 27.

2 Martin Gilbert, *Auschwitz and the Allies* (New York: Holt, Rhinehart, and Winston, 1981), 233.

3 As one psychologist put it, "The sheer physical isolation of factory farms from the rest of society fulfills Bandura's (citation omitted) observation that harming others is made easier when their suffering is not visible." Hank Rothgerber, "Efforts to Overcome Vegetarian-induced Dissonance among Meat Eaters," *Appetite* 79 (2014), 33.

4 James Serpell, *In the Company of Animals: A Study of Human–Animal Relationships* (Cambridge: Cambridge University Press, 1986), 196.

5 Ibid.

6 Bandura called this form of willful blindness "selective inattention to harmful effects." Albert Bandura, *Moral Disengagement: How People Do Harm and Live with Themselves* (New York: Worth Publishers, 2016), 66.

7   Sune Borkfelt et al., "Closer to Nature? A Critical Discussion of the Marketing of 'Ethical' Animal Products," *Journal of Agricultural and Environmental Ethics* (28) (6) (2015), 1069.

8   In *The Omnivore's Dilemma*, Michael Pollan said that in the past people thought they could both honor and eat animals without looking away, but "nowadays it seems we either look away or become vegetarians." *The Omnivore's Dilemma: A Natural History of Four Meals* (New York: Penguin Press, 2006), 307.

9   Carolien Hoogland, Joop de Boer, and Jan Boersema, "Transparency of the Meat Chain in the Light of Food Culture and History," *Appetite* 45 (1) (2005), 16.

10 Arnold Arluke, "Getting into the Closet with Science: Information Control Among Animal Experimenters," *Journal of Contemporary Ethnography* 20 (3) (1991), 322.

11 Fort Knox is a secure vault in the United Staes where some of the country's gold reserves are kept.

12 Tara Holmberg and Malin Ideland, "Secrets and Lies: 'Selective Openness' in the Apparatus of Animal Experimentation," *Public Understanding of Science* 21 (3) (2012), 354.

13 Arluke, "Getting into the Closet," 322.

14 See Sarah Knight and Louise Barnett, "Justifying Attitudes Toward Animal Use: A Qualitative Study of People's Views and Beliefs," *Anthrozoös* 21 (1) (2008), 39.

15 One psychologist described factory farming as a taboo topic. Rothgerber, "Efforts to Overcome," 33, citing K. Iacobbo and M,. Iacobbo, *Vegetarians and Vegans in America Today* (Westport, Connecticut: Greenwood Publishing Group, 2006).

16 Kathryn Gillespie called the agreement between meat producers and consumers to avoid mentioning the process of slaughtering animals "silent collusion." Kathryn Gillespie, "How Happy Is Your Meat?: Confronting (Dis)connectedness in the 'Alternative' Meat Industry," *The Brock Review* 12 (1), 117.

17 Sahar Akhtar, "Animal Pain and Welfare: Can Pain Sometimes be Worse for Them than for Us?" in *The Oxford Handbook of Animal Ethics*, edited by Tom L. Beauchamp and R. G. Frey (Oxford: Oxford University Press, 2011), 495.

18 Benjamin Rush, "Observations Intended to Favour Supposition that the Black Color (as it is called) of the Negroes is derived from the Leprosy," *Transactions of the American Philosophical Society* (4) (1799), 192.
19 Akhtar, "Animal Pain and Welfare," 507.
20 Andrew Chignell, "Can We Really Vote with Our Forks?: Opportunism and the Threshold Chicken," in *Philosophy Comes to Dinner: Arguments About the Ethics of Eating*, edited by Andrew Chignell, Terence Cuneo, and Matthew C, Halteman (New York: Routledge, 2016), 184–202.
21 Steven McMullen, *Animals and the Economy*, (London: Palgrave Macmillan, 2016), 64.
22 Ibid., 65.
23 *New York Times,* May 18, 1997, C13; quoted in Peter Singer, *Ethics Into Action: Henry Spira and the Animal Rights Movement* (Lanham, Maryland: Rowman & Littlefield, 1998), 142–143.
24 The photo is from Singer, *Ethics Into Action*, 143, and is reproduced here with the author's permission.
25 Ruth Harrison, *Animal Machine: The New Factory Farming Industry* (Boston: CABI, 2013), 43.
26 John Robbins, *No Happy Cows: Dispatches from the Frontlines of the Food Revolution* (San Francisco: Conari Press, 2012), 23.
27 Matthew Cole, "From 'Animal Machines' to 'Happy Meat'? Foucault's Ideas of Disciplinary and Pastoral Power Applied to 'Animal-Centered' Welfare Discourse," *Animals* 1 (1) (2011), 94.
28 João Graca, Maria Manuela Calheiros, and Abílio Oliveira, "Moral Disengagement in Harmful but Cherished Food Practices? An Exploration into the Case of Meat," *Journal of Agricultural and Environmental Ethics* 27 (5) (2014), 759.
29 Ibid., 760.
30 Joan Dunayer, *Animal Equality: Language and Liberation* (Derwood, Maryland: Ryce Publishing, 2001), 119.
31 Ibid.
32 Brian Luke, *Brutal: Manhood and the Exploitation of Animals* (Urbana: University of Illinois Press, 2007), 74–75.

33 Rhiana Wegner at al., "Sexual Assault Perpetrators' Justifications for Their Actions: Relationships to Rape Supportive Attitudes, Incident Characteristics, and Future Perpetration," *Violence Against Women* 21 (8) (2015), 1020.

34 Kelly P. Dugan, "The 'Happy Slave' Narrative and Classics Pedagogy: A Verbal and Visual Analysis of Beginning Greek and Latin Textbooks," *New England Classical Journal* 46 (1) (2019), 63; Frederick Douglass, *Narrative of the Life of Frederick Douglass, an American Slave, Written by Himself* (Boston: Antislavery Office, 1845), 14–15.

Chapter 3: Denigrate the Victim

1 Primo Levi, *The Drowned and the Saved* (London: Joseph, 1988), 101; cited in Bandura, *Moral Disengagement: How People Do Harm and Live with Themselves* (New York: Worth Publishers, 2016), 88.

2 David Livingstone Smith, *Less Than Human: Why We Demean, Enslave, and Exterminate Others* (New York: St. Martin's Press, 2011), 11.

3 Richard Wrangham and Dale Peterson, *Demonic Males: Apes and the Origins of Human Violence* (Boston: Houghton Mifflin, 1996), 196; cited in James Waller, *Becoming Evil: How Ordinary People Commit Genocide and Mass Killing*, 2d ed. (Oxford: Oxford University Press, 2007), 220.

4 Alan Carter, "Animals, Pain and Morality," *Journal of Applied Philosophy* 22 (1) (2005), 17.

5 Working Party of the Institute of Medical Ethics, *Lives in the Balance: The Ethics of Using Animals in Biomedical Research*, edited by Jane A. Smith and Kenneth M. Boyd (Oxford: Oxford University Press, 1991), 66–67.

6 Susan Lederer, "Political Animals: The Shaping of Biomedical Research Literature in Twentieth Century America," *Isis* 83 (1) (1992), 73.

7 Roy Hendrickson, quoted in Deborah Blum, "Both Sides Using Moral Arguments," *Sacramento Bee*, November 24, 1991, A10; also quoted in Joan Dunayer, *Animal Equality: Language and Liberation* (Derwood, Maryland: Ryce Publishing, 2001), 114–115.

8   Mary Phillips, "Constructing Laboratory Animals: An Ethnographic Study in the Sociology of Science" (Ph.D. dissertation, New York University, 1991); quoted in Dunayer, *Animal Equality*, 115.

9   Consistent with their commodification, in 1988 oncomice were selected as a Product of the Year by *Fortune*. Fiona Murray, "The Oncomouse that Roared: Hybrid Exchange Strategies as a Source of Distinction at the Boundary of Overlapping Institutions," *Daedalus* 131 (2) (2002), 357.

10 According to the 3R principles of humane experimental technique put together by William Russell and Rex Burch, the production of animals designed to suffer from debilitating conditions is a form of direct inhumanity because it inflicts unavoidable distress on the animals. William Russell and Rex Burch, *The Principles of Humane Experimental Technique* (London: Methuen, 1959), 54.

11 L. J. Taylor, *National Hog Farmer* (March, 1978), 27; quoted in Peter Singer, *Animal Liberation* (New York: HarperCollins, 2009), 126.

12 J. Byrnes, "Raising Pigs by the Calendar at Maplewood Farm," *Hog Farm Management*, September 1976, 30; quoted in Jim Mason and Peter Singer, *Animal Factories: What Agribusiness Is Doing to the Family Farm, the Environment, and Your Health* (New York: Harmony Books, 1990), 1.

13 Jes Harfeld, "Husbandry to Industry: Animal Agriculture, Ethics and Public Policy," *Between the Species* 10 (8) (2010), 137.

14 Lauri Hyers, "Myths Used to Legitimize the Exploitation of Animals: An Application of Social Dominance Theory," *Anthrozoös* 19 (3) (2006), 200–201.

15 Daniel Goldhagen, *Hitler's Willing Executioners: Ordinary Germans and the Holocaust* (New York: Vintage Books, 1997), 176; quoted in David Sztybel, "Can the Treatment of Animals Be Compared to the Holocaust?" *Ethics and the Environment*, 11 (1) (2006), 112–113.

16 N. Taylor and H. Fraser, "Slaughterhouses: The Language of Life, the Discourse of Death," in *The Palgrave International Handbook of Animal Abuse Studies,* edited by Jennifer Maher, Harriet Pierpont, and Piers Beirne (London: Palgrave Macmillan, 2017), 193.

17 Arnold Arluke, "Sacrificial Symbolism in Animal Experimentation: Object or Pet?" *Anthrozoös* 2 (2) (1988), 101.

18 F. Peyton Rous, "Points to Look Out for in Connection with the Antivivisectionists" (undated memo listing the journal's publication guidelines); quoted in Dunayer, *Animal Equality*, 116.

19 James Serpell, *In the Company of Animals: A Study of Human–Animal Relationships* (Cambridge: Cambridge University Press,1996), 174.

20 Arnold Arluke, "Trapped in a Guilt Cage," *New Scientist* (April 4, 1992), 33.

21 Kathy Kellogg and Bob Kellogg, *Raising Pigs Successfully* (Charlotte, Vermont: Williamson, 1985), 13; quoted in Dunayer, *Animal Equality*, 141.

22 Gordon Allport, *The Nature of Prejudice* (Reading, Massachusetts: Addison-Wesley, 1979), 20.

23 Ibid., 23.

24 Boyka Bratanova, Steve Loughnan, and Brock Bastian, "The Effect of Categorization as Food on the Perceived Moral Standing of Animals," *Appetite* 57 (1) (2011), 195.

25 Brock Bastian et al., "Don't Mind Meat? The Denial of Mind to Animals Used for Human Consumption," *Personality and Social Psychology Bulletin* 38 (2) (2012), 247; Steve Loughnan, Brock Bastian, and Nick Haslam, "The Psychology of Eating Animals," *Current Directions in Psychological Science* 23 (2) (2014), 104.

26 Steve Loughnan, Nick Haslam, and Brock Bastian, "The Role of Meat Consumption in the Denial of Moral Status and Mind to Meat Animals," *Appetite* 55 (1) (2010), 156.

27 Jared Piazza and Steve Loughnan, "When Meat Gets Personal, Animals' Minds Matter Less: Motivated Use of Intelligence Information in Judgments of Moral Standing," *Social Psychological and Personality Science* 7 (8) (2016), 873.

28 Albert Bandura, Bill Underwood, and Michael E. Fromson, "Disinhibition of Aggression through Diffusion of Responsibility and Dehumanization of Victims," *Journal of Research in Personality* 9 (4) (1975), 253–269.

29 Philip G. Zimbardo, "A Situationist Perspective on the Psychology of Evil: Understanding How Good People Are Transformed into Perpetrators," in *The Social Psychology of Good and Evil*, edited by A. G. Miller (New York: Guilford Press, 2004), 32.

Chapter 4: Disparage Critics

1 W. Gilmore Simms, "The Morals of Slavery," in *The Pro-Slavery Argument* (Philadelphia: Lippincott & Grambo, 1853), 200.
2 Carl Cohen, "The Case for the Use of Animals in Biomedical Research," *The New England Journal of Medicine* 315 (14) (1986), 869.
3 Hank Rothgerber, "Efforts to Overcome Vegetarian-induced Dissonance among Meat Eaters," *Appetite* 79 (2014), 39.
4 Anthony Bourdain, *Kitchen Confidential: Adventures in the Culinary Underbelly* (New York: Bloomsbury, 2000), 70; quoted in Gordon Hodson, Kristof Dhont, and Megan Earle, "Devaluing Animals, 'Animalistic' Humans, and People Who Protect Animals," in *Why We Love and Exploit Animals: Bridging Insights from Academia and Advocacy*, edited by Kristof Dhont and Gordon Hodson (New York: Routledge, 2020), 81.
5 Julia Minson and Benoit Monin, "Do-Gooder Derogation: Disparaging Morally Motivated Minorities to Defuse Anticipated Reproach," *Social Psychological and Personality Science* 3 (2) (2012), 200.
6 Alina Salmen and Gordon Hodson, "Animalizing women and Feminizing (Vegan) Men: The Psychological Intersections of Sexism, Speciesism, Meat, and Masculinity," *Social and Personality Psychology Compass*, 17 (2), e12717.
7 Cara C. MacInnis and Gordon Hodson, "It Ain't Easy Eating Greens: Evidence of Bias Toward Vegetarians and Vegans from Both Source and Target," *Group Processes and Intergroup Relations* 20 (6) (2016), 12.
8 Ibid., 6.
9 Benedict de Spinoza, *Ethics*, translated by William H. White (New York: Macmillan, 1883), 209.
10 Roberta Kalechofsky, "Dedicated to Descartes' Niece: The Women's Movement in the Nineteenth Century and Anti-Vivisection," *Between the Species* 8 (2) (1992), 62.
11 Tara Holmberg and Malin Ideland, "Secrets and Lies: 'Selective Openness' in the Apparatus of Animal Experimentation," *Public Understanding of Science* 21 (3) (2012), 359.
12 Robert White, "Antivivisection: The Reluctant Hydra," *The American Scholar* 40 (3) (1971), 504.

13 Craig Buettinger, "Antivivisection and the Charge of Zoophil-psychosis in the Early Twentieth Century," *The Historian* 55 (2) (1995), 277.
14 Arnold Arluke, "Trapped in a Guilt Cage," *New Scientist* (4 April, 1992), 35.
15 Charles Griswold, Jr., "The Immorality of Animal Rights," *Washington Post*, January 5, 1986, D7, quoted by Adrian Morrison, "Making Choices in the Laboratory," in *Why Animal Experimentation Matters: The Use of Animals in Medical Research*, edited by Ellen Frankel Paul and Jeffrey Paul (New Brunswick, New Jersey: Transaction Publishers, 2001), 58.

Chapter 5: Displace Responsibility

1 *Trial of Adolph Eichmann, Record of Proceedings in the District Court of Jerusalem*, 29 June 1961, 4:1423.
2 Hank Rothgerber, "How We Love and Hurt Animals: Considering Cognitive Dissonance in Young Meat Eaters," in *Why We Love and Exploit Animals: Bridging Insights from Academia and Advocacy*, edited by Kristof Dhont and Gordon Hodson (New York: Routledge, 2020), 192.
3 Hein te Velde, Noelle Aarts, and Cees van Woerkum, "Dealing with Ambivalence: Farmers' and Consumers' Perceptions of Animal Welfare in Livestock Breeding," *Journal of Agricultural and Environmental Ethics* 15 (2) (2002), 214; Charlotte Schüßler et al., Moral Disengagement in the Media Discourses on Meat and Dairy Production Systems," *Appetite* 196 (107269) (2024), 7.
4 Jared Piazza et al., "Rationalizing Meat Consumption: The 4 Ns" *Appetite* 91 (2015), 116.
5 Joan Sabaté, "The Contribution of Vegetarian Diets to Health and Disease: A Paradigm Shift," *American Journal of Clinical Nutrition* 78 (supp.) (2003), 502S–507S.
6 W. J. Craig and A. R. Margelis, "Position of the American Dietetic Association: Vegetarian Diets," *Journal of the American Dietetic Association* 109 (7) (2009), 1266; see also Vesanto Melina, Winston Craig, and Susan Levin, "Position of the Academy of Nutrition and Dietetics: Vegetarian Diets," *Journal of the Academy of Nutrition and Dietetics* 116 (12) (2016), 1970.

7   Michael Pollan, *The Omnivore's Dilemma: A Natural History of Four Meals* (New York: Penguin Press, 2006), 310.
8   Carl Cohen, "The Case for the Use of Animals in Biomedical Research," *The New England Journal of Medicine* 315 (14) (1986), 868.

Chapter 6: Diffuse Responsibility

1   Robert Jay Lifton, *The Nazi Doctors: Medical Killing and the Psychology of Genocide* (New York: Basic Books, 1986), 450.
2   Jared Piazza et al., "Rationalizing Meat Consumption: The 4 Ns," *Appetite* 91 (2015), 124.
3   As the Scottish philosopher David Hume pointed out, it is a mistake to confuse *what is* with *what ought to be.* David Hume, *The Philosophical Works of David Hume,* volume II, edited by T. H. Green and T. H. Grose (London: Longmans, Green & Co., 1882), 245–246.
4   Milton Meltzer, *Slavery: A World History* (New York: Da Capo Press, 1993), 6.
5   Carl Cohen, "The Case for the Use of Animals in Biomedical Research," *The New England Journal of Medicine* 315 (14) (1986), 869.
6   Wesley Smith, *A Rat Is a Pig Is a Dog Is a Boy: The Human Cost of the Animal Rights Movement* (New York: Encounter Books, 2010), 198.
7   See David Wolfson, "Beyond the Law: Agribusiness and the Systemic Abuse of Animals," *Animal L.* 2 (1996), 123.
8   Iowa Code §717B. 3A (1).
9   Iowa Code §717B. 1 (1) (a), 717.1.4.

Chapter 7: The Exonerative Use of Comparisons

1   Christopher Browning, *Ordinary Men: Reserve Battalion 101 and the Final Solution in Poland* (New York: HarperCollins, 2017), 59.
2   Frank Minter, *The Politically Incorrect Guide to Hunting* (Washington, D.C.: Regnery Publishing, 2007), 13–14.
3   Wesley Smith, *A Rat Is a Pig Is a Dog Is a Boy: The Human Cost of the Animal Rights Movement* (New York: Encounter Books, 2010), 206.
4   Carl Cohen, "The Case for the Use of Animals in Biomedical Research," *The New England Journal of Medicine* 315 (14) (1986), 869.

5   Carl Cohen, "The Factual Setting of Animal Experimentation," in *The Animal Rights Debate*, edited by Carl Cohen and Tom Regan (Lanham, Maryland: Rowman & Littlefield, 2001), 14.

6   See Bandura, "Moral Disengagement in the Perpetration of Inhumanities," 195.

7   Seaton Baxter, *Intensive Pig Production: Environmental Management and Design* (London: Granada, 1984), 405; quoted in Joan Dunayer, *Animal Equality: Language and Liberation* (Derwood, Maryland: Ryce Publishing, 2001), 126.

8   Concerned that people may see the word *crate* in an unfavorable light, some in the industry suggested calling the enclosures *stalls* instead. C. C. Croney and R. D. Reynnells, "The Ethics of Semantics: Do We Clarify or Obfuscate Reality to Influence Perceptions of Farm Animal Production?" *Poultry Science* 87 (2) (2008), 389.

9   Russel R. Weisensel, letter, *Vealer USA,* July/August 1982, 24–25, at 25; quoted in Dunayer, *Animal Equality*, 127.

10 Erik Marcus, *Meat Market: Animals, Ethics, & Money* (Boston: Brio Press, 2005), 31.

Chapter 8: Moral Justification

1   Christopher Browning, *Ordinary Men: Reserve Battalion 101 and the Final Solution in Poland* (New York: Harper Collins, 2017), 73.

2   Albert Bandura, *Moral Disengagement: How People Do Harm and Live with Themselves* (New York: Worth Publishers, 2016), 58.

3   W. M. S. Russell and R. L. Burch, *The Principles of Humane Experimental Technique* (London: Methuen, 1959), 105.

4   Carl Cohen, "The Case for the Use of Animals in Biomedical Research," *The New England Journal of Medicine* 315 (14) (1986), 868.

5   Ibid., 869.

6   Ibid., 868.

7   Robert Bass, "Lives in the Balance: Utilitarianism and Animal Research." In *The Ethics of Animal Research: Exploring the Controversy,* edited by Jeremy R. Garrett (Cambridge, Massachusetts: MIT Press, 2012), 87.

8   Carl Cohen, "Rights and Interests," in *The Animal Rights Debate*, edited by Carl Cohen and Tom Regan (Lanham, Maryland: Rowman & Littlefield, 2001), 19.

9   David DeGrazia and Tom Beauchamp, "Beyond the 3 Rs to a More Comprehensive Framework of Principles for Animal Research Ethics," *ILAR Journal* 60 (3) (2019), 310.

10 Arianna Ferrari, "Contesting Animal Experiments through Ethics and Epistemology: In Defense of a Political Critique of Animal Experimentation," in *Animal Experimentation: Working Towards a Paradigm Change*, edited by Kathrin Hermann and Kimberley Jayne (Boston: Brill, 2019), 195.

11 Jerrold Tannenbaum, "The Paradigm Shift toward Animal Happiness: What It Is, Why It Is Happening, and What It Portends for Medical Research," in *Why Animal Experimentation Matters: The Use of Animals in Medical Research*, edited by Ellen Frankel Paul and Jeffrey Paul (New Brunswick, New Jersey: Transaction Publishers, 2001), 104.

12 Elizabeth Harman, "The Moral Significance of Animal Pain and Animal Death," in *The Oxford Handbook of Animal Ethics* (Oxford: Oxford University Press, 2011), 729; Christine Korsgaard, *Fellow Creatures: Our Obligations to Other Animals* (Oxford: Oxford University Press, 2018), 224.

13 David DeGrazia, "The Ethics of Confining Animals: From Farms to Zoos to Human Homes," in *The Oxford Handbook of Animal Ethics*, edited by Tom L. Beauchamp and R. G. Frey, 758; Elisa Galgut, "Raising the Bar in the Justification of Animal Research," *Journal of Animal Ethics* 5 (1) (2015), 10.

14 Scott Plous and Harold Herzog, "Reliability of Protocol Reviews for Animal Research," *Science* 293 (5530) (2001), 608.

15 Robert Bass, "Lives in the Balance: Utilitarianism and Animal Research," in *The Ethics of Animal Research: Exploring the Controversy*, edited by Jeremy R. Garrett (Cambridge, Massachusetts: MIT Press, 2012), 99.

16 Industrial livestock production operations are sometimes called Concentrated Animal Feeding Operations, or CAFOs.

17 Wesley J. Smith, *A Rat Is a Pig Is a Dog Is a Boy: The Human Cost of the Animal Rights Movement* (New York: Encounter Books, 2010), 210.

18 William Harper, "Harper's Memoir on Slavery," in *The Pro-slavery Argument* (Philadelphia: Lippincott, Grambo & Co., 1853), 88.

19 Lucas Reijnders and Sam Soret, "Quantification of the Environmental Impact of Different Dietary Protein Choices," *American Journal of Clinical Nutrition* 78 (supplement) (2003), 665S.

20 J. Poore and T. Nemecek, "Reducing Food's Environmental Impacts through Producers and Consumers," *Science* 363 (eaaw9908) (2018), 990.

21 Claus Leitzman, "Nutrition Ecology: The Contribution of Vegetarian Diets," *American Journal of Clinical Nutrition* 78 (3) (Supplement) (2003), 658S.

22 John Robbins, *Diet for a New America: How Your Food Choices Affect Your Health, Your Happiness, and the Future of Life on Earth* (Tiburon, California: H. J. Kramer, 2012), 327.

23 *The State of Food Security and Nutrition in the World 2022: Repurposing Food and Agricultural Policies to Make Healthy Diets More Affordable* (Rome: Food and Agriculture Organization of the United Nations, 2020), 30.

24 Leitzman, "Nutrition Ecology," 658S.

25 Tina H. T. Chin and Chin-Lon Lin, "Ethical Management of Food Systems: Plant-based Diet as a Holistic Approach," *Asia Pacific Journal of Clinical Nutrition* 18 (4) (2009), 650.

26 The Vegalog, "Cost of Living a Plant-Based Lifestyle," accessed on February 23, 2023, at https://voicelessindia.org/vegalog/f/cost-of-living-a-plant-based-lifestyle?blogcategory=Veganism.

27 Jonathan Safran Foer, *We Are the Weather: Saving the Planet Begins at Breakfast* (New York: Farrar, Straus, & Giroux, 2019), 166.

28 Cohen, "The Case for the Use of Animals in Biomedical Research," 867.

29 Ibid.

30 Ibid., 67.

31 Carl Cohen, "The Moral Inequality of Species," in *The Animal Rights Debate*, edited by Carl Cohen and Tom Regan, 62.

32 *Empathy* is defined as the ability to experience and share the feelings of others and respond with care to their distress. See Frans de Waal "Putting the Altruism Back into Altruism: The Evolution of Empathy," *Annual Review of Psychology* 59 (2008), 281; K. Z. Meyza et al., "The Roots of Empathy: Through the Lens of Rodent Models," *Neuroscience & Biobehavioral Reviews* 76 (2017), 216.

33 For our purposes, *altruism* is behavior that benefits a recipient at a cost to the actor. See de Waal, "Putting the Altruism Back into Altruism," 280.

34 For the following discussion, *morality* is a spectrum of behaviors motivated by a concern for the welfare of others, including providing help to them and not harming them. See Marc Bekoff and Jessica Pierce, *Wild Justice: The Moral Lives of Animals* (Chicago: The University of Chicago Press, 2009), 138.

35 Jun Chen. "Empathy for Distress in Humans and Rodents," *Neuroscience Bulletin* 34 (1) (2018): 219.

36 Inbal Ben-Ami Bartal, Jean Decety, and Peggy Mason, "Empathy and Pro-Social Behavior in Rats," *Science* 334 (6061) (2011), 1427–1430.

37 Ushnik Das et al., "Demonstration of Altruistic Behaviour in Rats," *bioRxiv* 805481 (2019).

38 Showing the moral dexterity that Albert Bandura mentioned in this chapter's introductory quotation, the discovery that rats have the capacity for altruism didn't lead researchers to stop using them in experiments. Instead, some performed experiments that successfully induced deficits in their prosocial behavior by socially isolating them from others after they had been weaned [Áron Tulogdi et al., "Effects of Resocialization on Post-Weaning Social Isolation-Induced Abnormal Aggression and Social Deficits in Rats," *Developmental Psychobiology* 56 (1) (2014), 49–57] or damaging their amygdala, an area of the brain thought to be responsible for affiliative emotions and behavior [Julen Hernandez-Lallement et al., "Basolateral Amygdala Lesions Abolish Mutual Reward Preferences in Rats," *Neurobiology of Learning and Memory* 127 (2016), 1–9]. The goal was to create a cheap, convenient, and ethically less controversial animal model of callousness than

using non-human primates [Julen Hernandez-Lallement, Marijn van Wingerden, and Tobias Kalenscher, "Towards an Animal Model of Callousness," *Neuroscience and Biobehavioral Reviews* 91 (2018), 124]. Human models were close at hand.

39 Dale Langford et al., "Social Modulation of Pain as Evidence for Empathy in Mice," *Science* 312 (5782) (2006), 1969; Hiroshi Ueno et al., "Empathic Behavior According to the State of Others in Mice," *Brain and Behavior* 8 (7) (2018), e00986.

40 de Waal, "Putting the Altruism Back into Altruism," 288.

41 Stanley Wechkin, Jules Masserman, and William Terris, Jr., "Shock to a Conspecific as an Aversive Stimulus," *Psychonomic Science* 64 (1-12P) (1964), 47–48.

42 Frans de Waal, "Morally Evolved: Primate Social Instincts, Human Morality, and the Rise and Fall of 'Veneer Theory,'" in *Primates and Philosophers: How Morality Evolved*, edited by Stephen Macedo and Josiah Ober (Princeton, New Jersey: Princeton University Press, 2006), 29.

43 Ana Pérez-Manrique and Antoni Gomila, "The Comparative Study of Empathy: Sympathetic Concern and Empathic Perspective-taking in Non-human Animals," *Biological Reviews* 93 (1) (2017), 248–69.

44 Sivaani Sivaselvachandran et al., "Behavioral and Mechanistic Insight into Rodent Empathy," *Neuroscience and Biobehavioral Reviews* 91 (2018), 131.

45 David DeGrazia, *Taking Animals Seriously: Mental Life and Moral Status* (Cambridge: Cambridge University Press, 1996), 204.

46 Bekoff and Pierce, *Wild Justice: The Moral Lives of Animals*, 95–96.

47 Frans de Waal, "The Tower of Morality," in *Primates and Philosophers: How Morality Evolved,* edited by Stephen Macedo and Josiah Ober (Princeton, New Jersey: Princeton University Press, 2006), 181.

48 Keith Thomas, *Man and the Natural World: Changing Attitudes in England 1500–1800* (Oxford: Oxford University Press, 1983) 41; quoted in James Serpell, *In the Company of Animals: A Study of Human-Animal Relationships* (Cambridge: Cambridge University Press, 1986), 170.

49 Letter, Descartes to Henry More, 5 February 1649, in *Oeuvres de Descartes* (1903), 5:275; quoted in Paul Friedland, "Friends for Dinner: The Early Modern Roots of Modern Carnivorous Sensibilities," *History of the Present: A Journal of Critical History* 1 (1) (2011), 89.

50 Brock Bastian and Steve Loughnan, "Resolving the Meat-Paradox: A Motivational Account of Morally Troubling Behavior and Its Maintenance," *Personality and Social Psychology Review* 21 (3) (2016), 281.

51 Frans de Waal, *Are We Smart Enough to Know How Smart Animals Are?* (New York: W. W. Norton, 2016), 163.

52 Korsgaard, *Fellow Creatures*, 60.

53 See Karen Warren, "The Power and Promise of Ecological Feminism," *Environmental Ethics* 12 (2) (1990), 126-27.

54 According to de Waal, these candidates have included opposable thumbs, toolmaking, cooperative hunting, humor, pure altruism, sexual orgasm, the incest taboo, language, and the anatomy of the larynx. Frans de Waal, *Good Natured, The Origins of Right and Wrong in Humans and Other Animals* (Cambridge, Massachusetts: Harvard University Press, 1996), 65.

55 Frans de Waal, *Are We Smart Enough to Know How Smart Animals Are?*, 126.

56 Frans de Waal, *Are We Smart Enough to Know How Smart Animals Are?*, 107; Stephen Jay Gould, "The Human Difference," *New York Times,* July 2, 1999; Andrew Whiten, "The Burgeoning reach of Animal Culture," *Science* 372 (6537) (2021) eabe6514; de Waal, "The Tower of Morality," 181; For extended discussions about unfounded claims of human exceptionalism, please see Peter Marsh, *The Supremacist Syndrome: How Domination Underpins Slavery, Genocide, the Exploitation of Women and the Maltreatment of Animals* (Brooklyn, New York: Lantern Publishing and Media, 2021), 159–174.

57 Steve F. Sapontzis, "The Moral Significance of Interests," *Environmental Ethics* 4 (4) (1982), 345.

Chapter 9:
The Interconnection of Prejudices Against People and Animals

1. See *Understanding Prejudice and Discrimination*, edited by Scott Plous (New York: McGraw-Hill, 2003), 130, 531–532.
2. Ibid., 131, 532–533.
3. Gordon Allport, *The Nature of Prejudice* (Reading, Massachusetts: Addison-Wesley Publishing, 1979), 68.
4. Nazar Akrami, Bo Ekehammar, and Robin Bergh, "Generalized Prejudice: Common and Specific Components," *Psychological Science* 22 (1) (2011), 57.
5. Bob Altemeyer, "The Other 'Authoritarian Personality,'" in *Political Psychology*, edited by John J. Jost and Jim Sidanius (New York: Psychology Press, 2004), 90–92.
6. Martin Backström and Fredrik Björklund, "Structural Modeling of Generalized Prejudice: The Role of Social Dominance, Authoritarianism, and Empathy," *Journal of Individual Differences* 28 (1) (2007), 15.
7. Kristof Dhont, Gordon Hodson, and Ana L. Leite, "Common Ideological Roots of Speciesism and Generalized Ethnic Prejudice: The Social Dominance Human-Animal Relations Model (SD-HARM)," *European Journal of Personality* 30 (6) (2016), 516.
8. Taciano Lemos Milfont et al., "Environmental Consequences of the Desire to Dominate and Be Superior," *Personality and Social Psychology Bulletin* 39 (9) (2013), 1134.
9. See Lucius Caviola, Jim A. C. Everett, and Nadira S. Faber, "The Moral Standing of Animals: Towards a Psychology of Speciesism," *Journal of Personality and Social Psychology* 116 (6) (2019), 1026.
10. Gordon Allport's understanding that prejudiced beliefs and attitudes are overtly negative also needs to be updated in light of more recent research. As will be discussed later in this chapter, modern forms of prejudice include benevolent variants that are not openly negative but still serve to maintain a disfavored group's subordinate status. For our purposes, *prejudice* will be defined as ideologies, attitudes, and

beliefs that help maintain and legitimize group-based hierarchy and exploitation. Chris G. Sibley and Fiona Kate Barlow, "An Introduction to the Psychology of Prejudice," in *The Cambridge Handbook of The Psychology of Prejudice*, edited by Chris G. Sibley and Fiona Kate Barlow (Cambridge: Cambridge University Press, 2017), 3–4.

11 Scott Plous, "Is There Such a Thing as Prejudice Toward Animals?" in *Understanding Prejudice and Discrimination*, edited by Scott Plous, 509.

12 Kristof Dhont et al., "The Psychology of Speciesism," in *Why We Love and Exploit Animals: Bridging Insights from Academia and Advocacy*, edited by Kristof Dhont and Gordon Hodson (New York: Routledge, 2020), 29.

13 *Speciesism* is sometimes called *human supremacism* in the same way *racism* may be called *white supremacism* and *sexism* may be called *male supremacism*. Richard Ryder, a psychologist who coined the word *speciesism* in 1970, recognized later that over the years it had acquired different meanings. [Richard Ryder "Speciesism" in *Encyclopedia of Animal Rights and Animal Welfare*, edited by Marc Bekoff and Carron Meaney (Chicago: Fitzroy Dearborn, 1998), 320]. By now, it has acquired even more, some of which are morally neutral. For example, it can be defined as a preference for one's own kind. [*See* Shelly Kagan, "What's Wrong with Speciesism?" *Journal of Applied Philosophy* 33 (1) (2016), 3; and Frauke Albersmeier, "Speciesism and Speciescentrism," *Ethical Theory and Moral Practice* 24 (2021), 511–527]. Another morally neutral form of *speciesism* has been called *species-relativism,* the view that individuals should prioritize members of their own species because they have special relationships with them. [Lucius Caviola et al., "Humans First: Why People Value Animals Less than Humans," *Cognition* 225 (2022), 2]. Morally neutral definitions of *speciesism* have significantly reduced the term's value when discussing the morality of human exceptionalism. Group favoritism becomes morally objectionable when combined with a belief that one's own group is superior to all others and entitled to dominate and exploit members

of "inferior" groups. *Human supremacism* expresses this idea more simply and clearly than *speciesism* and will be used when referring to an ideology that includes such a belief.

14 Caviola, Everett, and Faber, "The Moral Standing of Animals;" 1026; Kristof Dhont et al., "The Psychology of Speciesism," 35; Lynne M. Jackson, *The Psychology of Prejudice: From Attitudes to Social Action*, 2d ed. (Washington, D.C.: American Psychological Association, 2020), 199.

15 Dhont et al., "The Psychology of Speciesism," in *Why We Love and Exploit Animals*, 29.

16 Marjorie Spiegel, *The Dreaded Comparison: Human and Animal Slavery* (New York: Mirror Books, 1996); Carol J. Adams, *The Sexual Politics of Meat: A Feminist-Vegetarian Critical Theory* (New York: Continuum, 1996); Plous, "Is There Such a Thing as Prejudice Toward Animals?" 510–511.

17 Caviola, Everett, and Faber, "The Moral Standing of Animals," 1018.

18 Backström and Björklund, "Structural Modeling of Generalized Prejudice: The Role of Social Dominance, Authoritarianism, and Empathy," 13; Caviola, Everett, and Faber, "The Moral Standing of Animals," 1020.

19 Faith Uenal et al., "The Roots of Ecological Dominance Orientation: Assessing Individual Preferences for an Anthropocentric and Hierarchically Organized World," *Journal of Environmental Psychology* 81 (2022) 101783, 11.

20 Caviola, Everett, and Faber, "The Moral Standing of Animals," 1020.

21 David Livingstone Smith, *Less Than Human: Why We Demean, Enslave, and Exterminate Others* (New York: St. Martin's Press, 2011), 11.

22 See *Understanding Prejudice and Discrimination*, edited by Plous, 510; Gordon Hodson and Kristof Dhont, "An Integrated Psychology of (Animalistic) Dehumanization Requires a Focus on Human-Animal Relations," *Current Research in Ecological and Social Psychology* 5 (2023), 100131.

23 Jackson, *The Psychology of Prejudice*, 190–191.

24 Brock Bastian et al., "Don't Mind Meat? The Denial of Mind to Animals Raised for Human Consumption," *Personality and Social Psychology Review* 38 (2) (2012), 253–254; Caviola, Everett, and Faber, "The Moral Standing of Animals," 1013–1014.

25 Boyka Bratanova, Steve Loughnan, and Brock Bastian, "The Effect of Categorization as Food on the Perceived Moral Standing of Animals," *Appetite* 57 (1) (2011), 195–196.

26 Bastian et al., "Don't Mind Meat?," 254.

27 Joan Dunayer, "Sexist Words, Speciesist Roots," in *Animals and Women: Feminist Theoretical Explorations*, edited by Carol J. Adams and Josephine Donovan (Durham, North Carolina: Duke University Press, 1995), 12–15.

28 Catharine A. MacKinnon, "Of Mice and Men: A Feminist Fragment on Animal Rights," in *Animal Rights: Current Debates and New Directions*, edited by Cass R. Sunstein and Martha C. Nussbaum (Oxford: Oxford University Press, 2004), 265.

29 Felicia Pratto et al., "Social Dominance Orientation: A Personality Variable Predicting Social and Political Attitudes," *Journal of Personality and Social Psychology* 67 (4) (1994), 748–749.

30 Bob Altemeyer, "The Other 'Authoritarian Personality,'" 100.

31 Dhont, Hodson, and Leite, "Common Ideological Roots of Speciesism and Generalized Prejudice," 517.

32 Milfont et al., "Environmental Consequences of the Desire to Dominate and Be Superior," 1134; Taciano Milfont et al., "On the Relation between Social Dominance Orientation and Environmentalism: A 25-Nation Study," *Social Psychological and Personality Science* 9 (7) (2018), 810.

33 Faith Uenal et al., "The Roots of Ecological Dominance Orientation," 101783.

34 Ibid.

35 Ibid.

36 Nour S. Kteily and Jennifer A. Richardson, "Perceiving the World through Hierarchy-shaped Glasses: On the Need to Embed Social Identity Effects on Macro-level Social Inequality and Violence across

Societies." *Psychological Inquiry* 27 (4) (2016), 327; Faith Uenal, Jim Sidanius, and Sander van der Linden, "Social and Ecological Dominance: Two Sides of the Same Coin? Social and Ecological Dominance Orientations Predict Decreased Support for Climate Change Mitigation Policies," *Group Processes and Intergroup Relations* 25 (6) (2022), 1557.

37 As Lynne Jackson put it in the second edition of her textbook on prejudice ". . . it is faulty understandings of nonhuman animals as qualitatively and substantively different from humans that makes it possible to degrade them. By implication, people can be degraded by comparing them with animals." Jackson, *The Psychology of Prejudice*, 196.

38 Smith, *Less Than Human: Why We Demean, Enslave, and Exterminate Others*, 42.

39 David Livingstone Smith, "Paradoxes of Dehumanization," *Social Theory and Practice* 42 (2) (2016), 416.

40 Jackson, *The Psychology of Prejudice*, 196.

41 Melvin Drimmer, "Thoughts on the Persistence of American Racism," *The History Teacher* 4 (3) (1970), 18; quoted in Plous, *Understanding Prejudice and Discrimination*, 125.

42 See Felicia Pratto et al., "Social Dominance Orientation: A Personality Variable Predicting Social and Political Attitudes," 743.

43 Felicia Pratto et al., "Social Dominance Orientation and the Legitimization of Inequality Across Cultures," *Journal of Cross-Cultural Psychology* 31 (3) (2000), 379.

44 Gustave Le Bon, *Revue d'Anthropologie*, 1879; quoted in Stephen Jay Gould, "Women's Brains," in *The Panda's Thumb: More Reflections in Natural History* (New York: W. W. Norton, 1980), 155; quoted in Plous, *Understanding Prejudice*, 224.

45 Glick and Fiske, "An Ambivalent Alliance," 109–118.

46 Jackson, *The Psychology of Prejudice*, 97.

47 Richard P. Haynes, "The Myth of Happy Meat," *The Philosophy of Food* 39 (2012), 161–168.

48 Michael Pollan, *The Omnivore's Dilemma: A Natural History of Four Meals* (New York: Penguin Press, 2006*)*, 328.

49 Philip C. Glatz and Greg Underwood, "Current Methods and Techniques of Beak Trimming Laying Hens, Welfare Issues and Alternative Approaches," *Animal Production Science* 61 (10) (2020), 968–989.

50 J. Fournier at al., "The Effect of Toe Trimming on Behavior, Mobility, Toe Length and Other Indicators of Welfare in Tom Turkeys," *Poultry Science* 94 (7) (2015), 1452.

51 Livestock Conservancy, "Definition of a Heritage Turkey," accessed April 2, 2022, at https://livestockconservancy.org/index.php/resources/internal/heritage-turkey.

52 John Robbins, "The Truth About Grassfed Beef," accessed August 7, 2022, at https://foodrevolution.org/blog/the-truth-about-grassfed-beef/.

53 Elizabeth Harman, "The Moral Significance of Animal Pain and Animal Death," in *The Oxford Handbook of Animal Ethics*, edited by Tom Beauchamp and R. G. Frey (Oxford: Oxford University Press, 2011), 729.

54 Donna Marie Artuso, "A Language and Messaging Guide for Scientists Discussing Humane, Responsible Animal Research," accessed April 2, 2022, at https://www.toxicology.org/pubs/docs/air/LanguageMessagingGuide.pdf.

55 Cambridge English Dictionary, accessed January 23, 2023, at https://dictionary.cambridge.org/us/dictionary/english/humane.

56 Nathan Nobis, "Carl Cohen's 'Kind' Arguments *For* Animal Rights and *Against* Human Rights," *Journal of Applied Philosophy* 21 (1) (2004), 43.

57 Tom L. Beauchamp and David DeGrazia, *Principles of Animal Research Ethics* (Oxford: Oxford University Press, 2020), ix.

58 William M. S. Russell and Rex L. Burch, *The Principles of Humane Experimental Technique* (London: Methuen, 1959), 155.

59 Ibid., 25.

60 David DeGrazia, "The Ethics of Confining Animals: From Farms to Zoos to Human Homes," in *The Oxford Handbook of Animal Ethics*, edited by Tom L. Beauchamp and R. G. Frey (Oxford: Oxford University Press, 2011), 738.

61 Ibid., 5.

Chapter 10: Overcoming Interconnected Prejudices

1 Kristof Dhont et al., "The Psychology of Speciesism," in *Why We Love and Exploit Animals: Bridging Insights from Academia and Advocacy* (New York: Routledge, 2020), 35–36.

2 Bob Altemeyer, "The Other 'Authoritarian Personality,'" in *Political Psychology: Key Readings in Social Psychology,* edited by John T. Jost and Jim Sidanius (New York: Psychology Press, 2004), 85–107; Nour Kteily, Arnold K. Ho, and Jim Sidanius, "Hierarchy in the Mind: The Predictive Power of Social Dominance Orientation across Social Contexts and Domains," *Journal of Experimental Social Psychology* 48 (2) (2012), 547–548; Kristof Dhont, Gordon Hodson, and Ana L. Leite, "Common Ideological Roots of Speciesism and Generalized Prejudice: The Social Dominance Human–Animal Relations Model (SD-HARM)," *European Journal of Personality* 30 (2016), 517; Lucius Caviola, Jim A. C. Everett, and Nadira S. Faber, "The Moral Standing of Animals: Towards a Psychology of Speciesism," *Journal of Personality and Social Psychology* 116 (6) (2018), 1020.

3 A 2011 study found that support for social dominance includes two aspects: the preference for some groups' dominating others and a complementary preference for non-egalitarian intergroup relations. The preference for dominance seems to be associated with overt prejudice and oppression by a dominant group, while support for group-based inequality appears associated with more covert forms of prejudice and support for the maintenance of social inequality. Arnold K. Ho et al., "Social Dominance Orientation: Revisiting the Structure and Function of a Variable Predicting Social and Political Attitudes," *Personality and Social Psychology Bulletin* 38 (5) (2011), 595.

4 Altemeyer, "The Other 'Authoritarian Personality,'" 91; Sam McFarland, "Authoritarianism, Social Dominance, and Other Roots of Generalized Prejudice," *Political Psychology* 31 (3) (2010), 456.

5 John Duckitt and Chris G. Sibley, "The Dual Process Motivational Model of Ideology and Prejudice," in *The Cambridge Handbook of the Psychology of Prejudice*, edited by Chris G. Sibley and Fiona Kate Barlow (Cambridge: Cambridge University Press, 2017), 192.

6   Martin Backström and Fredrik Björklund, "Structural Modeling of Generalized Prejudice: The Role of Social Dominance, Authoritarianism, and Empathy," *Journal of Individual Differences* 28 (1) (2007), 16; McFarland, "Authoritarianism, Social Dominance, and Other Roots of Generalized Prejudice," 470.

7   Ibid., 459.

8   Backström and Björklund, "Structural Modeling of Generalized Prejudice," 15–16.

9   Jim Sidanius, B. J. Cling, and Felicia Pratto, "Ranking and Linking as a Function of Sex and Gender Role Attitudes," *Journal of Social Issues* 47 (3) (1991), 140.

10 Stylianos Syropoulos et al., " Bigotry and the Human–Animal Divide: (Dis)Belief in Human Evolution and Bigoted Attitudes Across Different Cultures," *Journal of Personality and Social Psychology* (2022), 24.

11 Ibid., 25.

12 Ibid., 12.

13 Intergroup contact may reduce prejudice by showing that the groups are more similar than previously thought, that beliefs about a categorical difference between them is mistaken.

14 See Lynne M. Jackson, *The Psychology of Prejudice: From Attitudes to Social Action*, 2d ed. (Washington, D.C.: American Psychological Association, 2020), 196.

15 The Aristotelian principle that equals should be treated equally and unequals unequally has been called the most fundamental principle of justice. Manual Velasquez et al., "Justice and Fairness," *Issues in Ethics* 3 (2) (1990), 2.

16 Marc Bekoff and Jessica Pierce, *Wild Justice: The Moral Lives of Animals* (Chicago: University of Chicago Press, 2010), 49.

17 Frans de Waal, *Are We Smart Enough to Know How Smart Animals Are?* (New York: W. W. Norton, 2016), 12.

18 Briefly stated, the "logic" of supremacist ideologies goes this way: (1) They are different from us; (2) That difference makes them inferior to us; and (3) Their inferiority makes it alright for us to dominate and exploit them.

19 *See* Lynne M. Jackson and Aaron Gibbings, "Social Dominance and Legitimizing Myths About Animal Use," *Anthrozoös* 29 (1) (2015), 158; Gordon Hodson and Kristof Dhont, "An Integrated Psychology of (Animalistic) Dehumanization Requires a Focus on Human–Animal Relations," *Current Research in Ecological and Social Psychology* (2023): 100131, 4.

20 Hodson and Dhont, "An Integrated Psychology of (Animalistic) Dehumanization Requires a Focus on Human–Animal Relations," 4.

21 Dhont, "The Psychology of Speciesism," 41.

22 David Nibert, *Animal Rights/Human Rights: Entanglements of Oppression and Liberation* (Boulder, Colorado: Rowman and Littlefield, 2002), 4; Carol L. Glasser, "Tied Oppressions: An Analysis of How Sexist Imagery Reinforces Speciesist Sentiments," *The Brock Review* 12 (1) (2011), 53.

23 Emily Gaarder, "Where the Boys Aren't: The Predominance of Women in Animal Rights Activism," *Feminist Formations* 23 (2) (2011), 60.

24 Dorceta E. Taylor, "Gender and Racial Diversity in Environmental Organizations: Uneven Accomplishments and Cause for Concern," *Environmental Justice* 8 (5) (2015), 166; Karen Bell, "Bread and Roses: A Gender Perspective on Environmental Justice and Public Health," *International Journal of Environmental Research and Public Health* 13 (10) (2016), 1005.

25 Belinda Robnett, "African-American Women in the Civil Rights Movement, 1954–1965: Gender, Leadership, and Micromobilization," *American Journal of Sociology* 101 (6) (1996), 1670–1672.

26 Glasser, "Tied Oppressions," 51.

27 Kimberly Christensen, "'With Whom Do You Believe Your Lot Is Cast?' White Feminists and Racism," *Signs: Journal of Women in Culture and Society* 22 (3) (1997), 629–630.

28 Sue Ellen Brown, "The Under-representation of African American Employees in Animal Welfare Organizations in the United States," *Society and Animals* 13 (2) (2005), 157; Michelle Rojas-Soto,

"Oppression Without Hierarchy: Racial Justice and Animal Advocacy," in *Antiracism in Animal Advocacy: Igniting Cultural Transformation*, edited by Jasmin Singer (Brooklyn: Lantern Publishing & Media, 2021), 145–146.

29 Taylor, "Gender and Racial Diversity in Environmental Organizations," 167.

30 For information about the funding each country provides to the U.N. Environment Programme, see https://www.unep.org/about-un-environment/funding-and-partnerships/check-your-contributions?_ga=2.260100813.1913759766.1699807508-989401027.1693253827.

31 Jim Sidanius and Felicia Pratto, *Social Dominance: An Intergroup Theory of Social Hierarchy and Oppression* (Cambridge: Cambridge University Press, 1999), 36.

32 Lise Eliot, "Brain Development and Physical Aggression: How a Small Gender Difference Grows into a Violence Problem," *Current Anthropology* 62 (S23) (2021), S566.

33 Matthew Guttman, "The Animal Inside: Men and Violence," *Current Anthropology* 62 (S23) (2021), S182.

34 Minou Ella Mebane, Antonio Aiello, and Donata Francescato, "Political Gender Gap and Social Dominance Orientation," in *Psycho-Social Aspects of Human Sexuality and Ethics*, edited by Dhastagir Sheriff (London: IntechOpen, 2020), 10.

35 Albert Bandura, "Selective Moral Disengagement in the Exercise of Moral Agency," *Journal of Moral Education* 31 (2) (2002), 115.

36 Marinella Paciello et al., "Stability and Change of Moral Disengagement and Its Impact on Aggression and Violence in Late Adolescence," *Child Development* 79 (5) (2008), 1296.

37 Only six nations have failed to ratify or accede to the Convention: Iran, Palau, Somalia, Sudan, Tonga, and the United States.

38 For example, 178 countries maintain legal barriers that prevent women's full economic participation. "Sustainable Development Goals Goal 5: Achieve gender equality and empower all women and girls," United Nations (2023), accessed on September 30, 2023, at https://www.un.org/sustainabledevelopment/gender-equality/.

39 Jeni Klugman and Beatrice Duncan, "Shaping the Law for Women and Girls: Experiences and Lessons from UN Women's Interventions (2015-2020)," UN Women (2022), 11. Accessed on October 8, 2023, at https://www.unwomen.org/sites/default/files/2022-01/Shaping-the-law-for-women-and-girls-en.pdf.

40 United Nations Sustainable Development Goals – Goal 5.

41 Article 21 of the Universal Declaration of Human Rights, United Nations General Assembly Resolution 217, December 10, 1948.

42 You can see your country's 2022 contribution to UN Women at https://www.unwomen.org/en/digital-library/publications/2023/09/regular-resources-report-2022.

43 Boris Bizumic and John Duckitt, "What Is and Is Not Ethnocentrism? A Conceptual Analysis and Political Implications," *Political Psychology* 33 (6), 902.

44 Ibid., 889.

45 John Williams, Deborah Best, and Donna Boswell, "The Measurement of Children's Racial Attitudes in the Early School Years," *Child Development* 46 (1975), 498.

46 Gordon Allport, *The Nature of Prejudice* (Reading, Massachusetts: Addison-Wesley Publishing, 1979), 281.

47 Thomas F. Pettigrew and Linda R. Tropp, "A Meta-Analytic Test of Intergroup Contact Theory," *Journal of Personality and Social Psychology* 90 (5) (2006), 751–783.

48 Ibid., 764.

49 Marie-Louise Mares and Zhongdang Pan, "Effects of *Sesame Street*: A Meta-analysis of Children's Learning in 15 Countries," *Journal of Applied Developmental Psychology* 34 (3) (2013), 148.

50 Mordechai Gordon, "Multicultural Education: Moving Beyond Heroes and Holidays," *Education for Meaning and Social Justice* 17 (4) (2004), 32.

Appendix

1 Michael Pollan, *The Omnivore's Dilemma: A Natural History of Four Meals* (New York: Penguin Press, 2006), 309, 319.

2 Ibid., 319.

3   See Peter Marsh, *The Supremacist Syndrome: How Domination Underpins Genocide, Slavery, the Exploitation of Women and the Maltreatment of Animals* (Brooklyn, New York: Lantern Publishing & Media, 2021), 188–196.

4   Michael Pollan, "An Animal's Place," *New York Times Magazine*, November 10, 2002, accessed December 10, 2023, at https://www.nytimes.com/2002/11/10/magazine/an-animal-s-place.html.

5   Henning Steinfeld et al., *Livestock's Long Shadow: Environmental Issues and Options,* Rome: Food and Agriculture Organization of the United Nations (2006).

6   Ibid., xx.

7   Ibid., xxii.

8   Ibid., 114.

9   David Pimentel and Marcia Pimentel, "Sustainability of Meat-based and Plant-based Diets and the Environment," *American Journal of Clinical Nutrition* 78 (supp.) (2003), 662S.

10 Steinfeld et al., *Livestock's Long Shadow,* xxii.

11 Ibid., xxiii.

12 Ibid., xxi.

13 Nathan Pelletier, Rich Pirog, and Rebecca Rasmussen, "Comparative Life-cycle and Environmental Impacts of Three Beef Production Strategies in the Upper Midwestern United States," *Agricultural Systems* 103 (2010), 386.

14 Sean Clark, "Organic Farming and Climate Change: The Need for Innovation," *Sustainability* 2020 (12) (2020), 7012.

15 "Big Meat and Dairy's Supersized Climate Footprint," *Climate* (November 7, 2017), accessed on December 16, 2023, at https://grain.org/article/entries/5825-big-meat-and-dairy-s-supersized-climate-footprint.

16 Luca Fernando Ruini et al., "Working toward Healthy and Sustainable Diets: The 'Double Pyramid Model' Developed by the Barilla Center for Food and Nutrition to Raise Awareness about the Environmental and Nutritional Impact of Foods," *Frontiers in Nutrition*, 2: 9 (May, 2015), 3.

17 Peter Singer and Jim Mason, *The Ethics of What We Eat: Why Our Food Choices Matter* (New York: Rodale, 2007), 28.
18 Wesley J. Smith, *A Rat Is a Pig Is a Dog Is a Boy: The Human Cost of the Animal Rights Movement* (New York: Encounter Books, 2010), 210.
19 Accessed on March 15, 2021, at https://www.worldstopexports.com/animal-feeds-exporters-by-country/
20 Accessed on March 10, 2021, at https://www.nationalheraldindia.com/india/global-hunger-index-2020-india-ranks-94-among-107-countries.
21 *The State of the World's Fisheries and Aquaculture 2020: Sustainability in Action* (Rome: Food and Agriculture Organization of the United Nations, 2020), 2.
22 Jonathan Balcombe, *What a Fish Knows: The Inner Lives of Our Underwater Cousins* (New York: Farrar, Straus, and Giroux, 2016), 216
23 Victoria Braithwaite, *Do Fish Feel Pain?* (Oxford: Oxford University Press, 2010), 18.
24 Balcombe, *What a Fish Knows,* 219.
25 Ibid.
26 Jonathan Safran Foer, *Eating Animals* (New York: Back Bay Books, 2009), 193.
27 Michael Pollan, *The Omnivore's Dilemma*, 313.
28 Ibid., 317–318.
29 Neville G. Gregory, *Animal Welfare and Meat Production* (Wallingford, Oxfordshire: CABI Publishing, 2007), 122.
30 John Webster, *Animal Welfare: A Cool Eye Towards Eden* (Oxford: Blackwell Publishing, 1994), 157.

About the Author

Peter Marsh secured a bachelor's degree in psychology from Wesleyan University in 1976. After receiving a law degree four years later, he represented people with disabilities and organizations that provide services to them. He also helped humane organization rescue groups, animal care and control agencies, and foundations establish effective animal shelter overpopulation programs in communities throughout the United States.

About the Publisher

Lantern Publishing & Media was founded in 2020 to follow and expand on the legacy of Lantern Books—a publishing company started in 1999 on the principles of living with a greater depth and commitment to the preservation of the natural world. Like its predecessor, Lantern Publishing & Media produces books on animal advocacy, veganism, religion, social justice, humane education, psychology, family therapy, and recovery. Lantern is dedicated to printing in the United States on recycled paper and saving resources in our day-to-day operations. Our titles are also available as ebooks and audiobooks.

To catch up on Lantern's publishing program, visit us at www.lanternpm.org.

facebook.com/lanternpm
instagram.com/lanternpm
tiktok.com/@lanternpmofficial